WHO THINKS? WHO BREATHES?

Reflections on the *Kena Upanishad*

VIVEK DESAI

Includes original Sanskrit, transliteration, and English translation.

Published by
Shanti Mandir, Inc.
51 Muktananda Marg, Walden, NY 12586
United States of America

Telephone: 845-778-1008
Email: walden@shantimandir.com
Website: www.shantimandir.com

Cover photograph: Shanti Mandir, Walden, NY,
by Ron Carter

ISBN 978-1-7321420-3-9

First edition: April 2018

Permissions appear in Acknowledgments on page 106.

COME, JOIN US as we listen in on this sublime conversation between an earnest seeker and a powerful Guru, in the hope that we, too, may unfold our human potential; discover true happiness; and live our lives more authentically, efficiently, and in harmony with everyone and everything around us.

– from the Introduction

Baba Muktananda

With countless prostrations,
dedicated to the lotus feet of Baba Muktananda,
who planted in me the seed of Self-knowledge,
who is the focus of my meditation,
who is God for me,
and who is the mirror in which I see my Self.

Photo: Ramakrishna Vitthal Gadekar

TABLE OF CONTENTS

TRANSLITERATION AND PRONUNCIATION GUIDE

IN THIS BOOK, Devanagari characters are transliterated according to the scheme adopted by the International Congress of Orientalists (ICO) at Athens in 1912. In this scheme, one fixed pronunciation value is given to each letter: f, q, w, x, and z are not called to use.

Note: All the sounds are only approximated in English words.

***svara* (vowels)**

अ a as in son
आ ā as in father
इ i as in if
ई ī as in feel
उ u as in full
ऊ ū as in boot
ऋ ṛ as in rhythm
ॠ ṝ as in reed
ऌ ḷ as in rlu
ॡ ḹ as in rlū
ए e as in evade
ऐ ai as in delight
ओ o as in core
औ au as in now

***anusvāra* (nasal)**

. ṁ as in improvise

visarga

: ḥ as in half h

***vyañjana* (consonants)**

***kaṇṭhya* (gutturals)**
from the throat

क् k as in calm
ख् kh as in blockhead
ग् g as in gate
घ् gh as in ghost
ङ् ṅ as in ankle

***tālavya* (palatals)**
with the middle of the tongue against the palate

च् c as in chuckle
छ् ch as in witch
ज् j as in justice
झ् jh as in hedgehog
ञ् ñ as in banyan

***mūrdhanya* (cerebrals)**
with the tip of the tongue against the roof of the mouth

ट् ṭ as in tank
ठ् ṭh as in anthill
ड् ḍ as in dog
ढ् ḍh as in adhesive
ण् ṇ as in under

***dantya* (dentals)**
with the tongue against the teeth

त् t as in with
थ् th as in thumb
द् d as in this
ध् dh as in breathe-here
न् n as in nose

***oṣṭhya* (labials)**
with the lips

प् p as in pen

फ् ph as in loophole

ब् b as in boil

भ् bh as in abhor

म् m as in mind

***antaḥstha* (semivowels)**

य् y as in yes

र् r as in right

ल् l as in love

व् v as in very

***ūṣma* (sibilants)**

श् ś as in shut

ष् ṣ as in sugar

स् s as in simple

***mahāprāṇa* (aspirate)**

ह् h as in happy

special conjunct consonants

क्ष् kṣ as in action

त्र् tr as in three

ज्ञ् jñ as in gnosis

avagraha

ऽ ' a silent 'a'

PREFACE

Why the *Kena Upaniṣad*?

THIS BOOK is not a traditional commentary on the *Kena Upaniṣad*—a sacred text on nonduality (*advaita*)—but might be better described as a compilation of my reflections on it.

The Sanskrit word *kena* means "by what?" or "by whom?" Essentially, it is interrogative in nature. This word deeply resonated with me because the spirit of questioning has always been natural to me. It was for this reason that I chose to pursue a degree in science. I was blessed to have excellent teachers train me in scientific method and research. I even went on to pursue a graduate degree in molecular biology. But I hit a brick wall—not externally, but internally. A deep conviction arose in me, triggered by a calling to wholeheartedly pursue the path of self-inquiry, that science is incapable of answering all questions in life. This was not disenchantment with science per se, but simply the realization of its limitations. For science—or any external pursuit, for that matter—cannot answer the existential question "What is the means to live a fulfilled life?"

Indeed, this inner quest had creeped in tangibly since the first year of my undergraduate college days. While I was pursuing science, I had a parallel pursuit in philosophy (first Western and then Indian), which soon expanded to include the practice of meditation. What triggered that expansion? The awakening is still fresh in my mind and heart.

It happened before beginning my second year as an undergraduate student. As an avid reader seeking the meaning of life, I had already turned to the sacred texts of the yoga tradition. Raised by a mother who is an ardent devotee of Baba Muktananda, the Guru of Gurus who created a "meditation revolution" in the 1970s and early 1980s, I was supremely blessed to grow up in an atmosphere of devotional love. However, obviously until a personal connection is made, one's worship remains distant and foreign. Having noticed my sincere seeking, my mother recommended I read Baba Muktananda's spiritual autobiography, *Play of Consciousness*. And I casually thought, "Why not?" Little did I know then that my life would never be the same again.

The person who finished reading that book was not the same as the one who started it. Baba Muktananda's words penetrated my being so deeply that it felt like taking a bath in the holiest of holy rivers. His worship of his Guru, the great *avadhūta* Bhagavan Nityananda of Ganeshpuri, touched a part of me that was so deep I did not even know existed. I didn't want the book to ever finish. I felt Baba was talking directly to me. I felt accepted, loved. I felt love that cannot be described in words. I felt complete. Tears welled up. There was nothing lacking in that experience. And most surprisingly, it felt so natural, nothing new or foreign. Baba's look and words ignited a deep longing within me to live in the state he lived in. I had never seen anyone like him—full of joy, totally free of any misery. I felt as if I were looking in a mirror, seeing what I can be and what I really am.

That heartfelt and visceral experience changed my life beyond what I could have imagined. What I had previously thought important dropped away. And things continue to drop away as I continue to unwrap that divine gift. I knew deep inside that Baba had answers to all the questions I was asking. I knew the path of meditation he pursued and so generously shared with the world is the means to find answers to the questions science, technology, and all external discoveries cannot answer. I knew the path of meditation alone could give the experience of fulfillment, not momentary sense pleasures or achievements.

The practice of meditation leads to an inquiry into one's true identity in order to find eternal happiness. This process is known as self-inquiry (*ātma-vicāra*). Because the word *kena* pointed to this profound secret, I could not help but enthusiastically embark on a deep exploration of this text in November 2016. Watching eloquent and lively lectures by Swami Chinmayananda, one of the great masters of the twentieth century, on this text further inspired me. I reveled in each word of this scripture, and found that each verse serves as a powerful pointer capable of catapulting the student into that state of wholeness or nonduality that is of the nature of peace, peace, and nothing but peace. It seemed too good not to share with others.

A series of opportunities allowed me to share the wisdom of the *Kena Upaniṣad* in public settings. First, I led an evening workshop at Hindu Temple of Delaware, and then led a month-long workshop series at Vitality Yoga in New Paltz, NY, both in the spring of 2017. These sharings allowed me to better formulate my reflections, which in turn deepened my understanding and experience of the scripture. The feedback—gauged not just by the verbal appreciation of the participants but also by the deep meditative silence palpable in the room—was so uplifting that penning my reflections and sharing them with a wider audience seemed the next natural step. The result of that is currently in your hands.

Due to the organic creation of this work, it should not be viewed as a commentary for academic study. Its purpose is not to satisfy intellectual curiosity but to inspire an experience of that divine supreme principle whose nature is eternal peace. I suggest pausing after each verse and reflecting on the impact of what has been shared. Many verses are followed by meditation exercises to engender a direct experience of the revelations. Given an opening, this timeless wisdom can completely transform our lives.

I pray to the Guru that this work may inspire every reader to inquire into his or her true nature and find peace within.

Shanti Mandir, Walden, NY
August 25, 2017, Ganesh Chaturthi

My mother (and grandmother) with our
Guru, Baba Muktananda, at Mumbai
Airport prior to departing for his
first world tour, 1970

Photo: my grandfather (Atul Dave)

INTRODUCTION

ANIMALS BUILD neither crematoriums nor houses of worship, which shows that they cannot reflect deeply on the nature of life, death, and beyond. What sets human apart from the rest of the animal kingdom? We carry out all the functions that most animals do: eating, sleeping, excreting, reproducing, and competing. But there is one unique human faculty that distinguishes us from them: the intellect (*buddhi*, or *viveka*, the power of discernment). The intellect allows us to reflect, to question, to inquire.

Animals	Humans
eat	eat
sleep	sleep
excrete	excrete
reproduce	reproduce
compete	compete
—	reflect

The scientific and the technological progress we have made, and even the very birth of civilization, owes its existence to this unique faculty of the intellect. To inquire about the external world enables progress in science, technology, art, politics, commerce, and trade. While advancement in the outer world certainly makes our lives comfortable, it does not provide contentment to the mind. Examples abound of personalities who have achieved tremendous success and fame in their respective fields, and even helped the world with their ingenious work, yet their personal lives remained plagued with stress and frustration, and in extreme cases, with anxiety and depression. Given this, what is the key to a satisfying life?

The wise beings of ancient India reflected deeply on this human condition, and discovered thousands of years ago that progress in the outer world is incomplete without an exploration of the inner world. The same intellect that allows us to explore the outer realms is capable of exploring the inner realms. While to investigate without is known as science, to do the same within is known as self-inquiry (ātma-vicāra, or *mananam*, reflection).

This time-tested practice can enable one to discover peace within oneself, allowing one to overcome inner turmoil and unlock enormous hidden potential. The *Upaniṣads* are conversations of self-inquiry in the ancient oral tradition between enlightened masters and sincere seekers, in which the nature of true identity is explored.

The *Upaniṣads* constitute the foundational sacred literature of Vedānta, one of the many living philosophical traditions of India. These sacred texts are thousands of years old. The date of their origin is subject to debate and can never truly be determined, for this wisdom was orally transmitted (*śruti*, that which is heard) from teacher to student before it was finally written down for posterity. Furthermore, its classification as śruti also shows that this wisdom was revealed to the sages (*ṛṣi*) in deep meditative states; thus, these texts are not products of any human mind but point to the eternal wisdom of nature that can be experienced by anyone at any time when the mind becomes silent. The ancients, therefore, did not bother to record the dates of these texts; for them, it was the wisdom contained therein that was important, not the date of writing, and not even the identity of the writer. The date of their origin might be ancient, but their wisdom is for all ages; the place of their origin might be the Indian subcontinent, but their wisdom is for all of humanity. Hence, this wisdom is known as *sanātana*—timeless and universal.

Ādi Śaṅkarācārya, the great sage-philosopher who lived around the eighth century CE, explains the word *upaniṣad* as made up of three words[1]: *upa*, which means "near"; *ni*, which means "steadfastness"; and *ṣad*, which has three meanings: "loosening of the ties," "propulsion (or knowledge)," and "complete destruction of all shackles." Thus, *upaniṣad* means the ultimate knowledge obtained by approaching (upa) an enlightened master with sincerity (ni); imbibing this knowledge provides an immediate sense of relief, and finally propels us to realization of our true nature, which destroys all attachments (ṣad), the root of

[1] Ādi Śaṅkarācārya explains the word *upaniṣad* in his introduction to the *Katha Upaniṣad.*

suffering. *Upaniṣad* is thus also the title given to a sacred text that explores this ultimate knowledge, the knowledge of our true nature.

Upaniṣad

upa = near
ni = steadfastness
ṣad = loosening of the ties,
knowledge,
complete destruction of all shackles

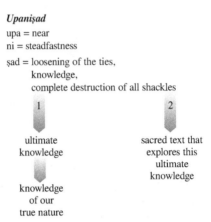

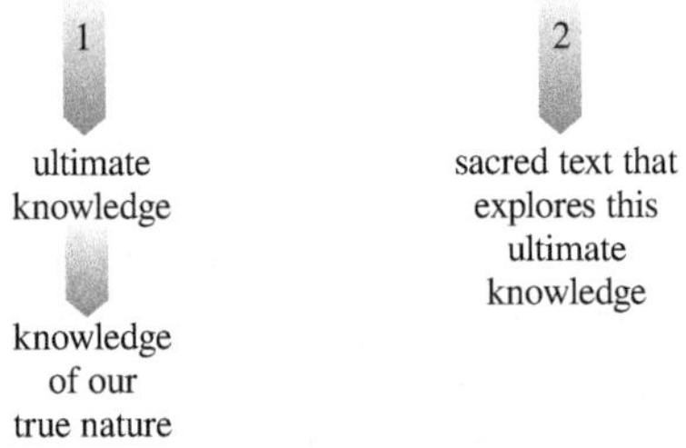

The *Upaniṣads* are classified as belonging specifically to the school of Advaita Vedānta, the nondual school within the philosophical tradition of Vedānta. *Advaita* means "not two [entities]," and *Vedānta* refers to the wisdom found at the "end portion (*anta*) of the *Vedas*."[2] The word *vedānta* can also be translated as the "end (anta) of all knowledge (*veda*)," meaning there is nothing higher than this knowledge of nonduality (advaita). Any other knowledge, any other information, in any field, is incomplete. In other words, a sense of complete fulfillment is experienced only when the wisdom of non-difference between oneself and the other dawns. This is not just the subject of all the *Upaniṣads* but is the true import of the word *upaniṣad*.

There are hundreds of *Upaniṣads*, and even though sadly many might have been lost (or may be even destroyed) over time, we fortunately still have enough available to guide us in our quest for

[2] *Vedas* are the sacred texts that form the foundation of Vedic or Hindu thought. They are accepted as the authority by all Vedic schools of thought.

eternal happiness. The *Kena Upaniṣad*, found in the *Sāma Veda*,[3] is one such *Upaniṣad*, classified as one of the ten principal *Upaniṣads,* and the only one on which Ādi Śaṅkarācārya wrote two commentaries. The title *Kena Upaniṣad* comes from the first word of the text: *kena* (by what? by whom?). The straightforwardness of this *Upaniṣad* is extraordinary. Its clarity is laser sharp. And its structure is enchanting, with the most notable feature being that both poetry (chapters one and two) and prose (chapters three and four) are included. Interestingly, lines are not drawn between personal and impersonal divinity.

This text provides a more effective approach than do psychiatry or psychotherapy for achieving mental balance. The divine is constantly pointed at but never described, and the key to interfaith harmony is given. The teacher tests the student by asking a question and tells a captivating story about gods and demons. The Goddess is invoked; nature meditations are explored; spiritual practice is visualized as a temple structure; practical tips for embodying the loftiest principles are offered; and most importantly, the message of nonduality is delivered without any compromise.

Come, join us as we listen in on this sublime conversation between an earnest seeker and a powerful Guru, in the hope that we, too, may unfold our human potential; discover true happiness; and live our lives more authentically, efficiently, and in harmony with everyone and everything around us.

[3] The *Sāma Veda* is one of the four *Vedas*, the other three being the *Ṛg Veda, Yajur Veda*, and *Atharva Veda*. The *Kena Upaniṣad* is also known as the *Talavakāra Upaniṣad* because it is part of the *Talavakāra Upaniṣad Brāhmaṇa* of the *Sāma Veda*.

INVOCATION

Mantras for Peace

Peace Mantra 1

ॐ सह नाववतु । सह नौ भुनक्तु । सह वीर्यं करवावहै ।
तेजस्विनावधीतमस्तु । मा विद्विषावहै ॥
ॐ शान्तिः शान्तिः शान्तिः

oṁ saha nāvavatu, saha nau bhunaktu, saha vīryaṁ karvāvahai,
tejasvināvadhītamastu, mā vidviṣāvahai.
oṁ śāntiḥ śāntiḥ śāntiḥ

Translation:
Oṁ. May that (divine) protect us both (teacher and student). May that (divine) nourish us both. May we work together with vitality. May our studies be bright. May we never hate each other.
Oṁ, peace, peace, peace.

THE STUDY of the *Upaniṣads* is not a mere intellectual endeavor. It cannot be understood by the mind alone; grace is essential. For this reason, each *Upaniṣad* begins with a śānti (peace) mantra[4] to invoke the blessings of the divine, the teachers, the sages, the gods, the ancestors, and the elders. *Kena Upaniṣad* has two śānti mantras.

"May that (divine) protect us both (teacher and student)."

The mantra begins by asking the divine for the protection of the Guru (a teacher who imparts Self-knowledge) and the disciple (a student of Self-knowledge); that is, for both the speaker and the listener. Since the divine dwells within all of us, the mantra also asks that we protect each other. An atmosphere of mutual trust and affection is conducive for the learning of any subject and for the growth of any student. Fear-based education creates a stressful environment, whereas affection-based education creates a stress-free environment.

[4] *Śānti* mantra or *śānti pāṭha*.

A truly transformative education requires a loving atmosphere, which the prayer here asks for.

"May that (divine) nourish us both."

While the first line addresses the fear within us, the second addresses the primal, biological desires within us. These are two of the primal urges that drive life: fear and desire. By pleading that the divine satisfy these urges in an uplifting way, the student here hopes to remain free of their distracting pull during the time of his higher studies. Even though the teacher is free of the pulls of the desires, the mantra prays that his basic needs of survival also be met without obstacles.

"May we work together with vitality."

Whereas the first two lines pray for mental health, this line prays for physical health. The body is the instrument through which spiritual practice (*sādhanā*) is carried out, so the health of the body is vital even for inner unfoldment. Sādhanā does not require the giving up of physical activity; on the contrary, it infuses one with enthusiasm to pursue one's daily tasks. The word *vīryam* is significant here because it means "vitality" or "vigor"; that is, not superficial muscle strength, but inner strength derived from self-discipline (*tapa*).

"May our studies be bright."

The *Upaniṣads* explore the most profound questions concerning life; for this reason, a sharp intellect is a must. The intellect needs to be bright so that it may not only understand the teachings intellectually but also know how to apply them in real life situations. Here it is asked that the teacher have a bright intellect to be able to interpret and convey the teachings, and that the student have a bright intellect to be able to understand and apply the teachings. This line asks for clarity of mind; in other words, intellectual health.

"May we never hate each other."

Until now, the prayer was focused on fine-tuning of one's personal being, and this last line is for harmony in interpersonal relationships. Conflict with others is more often than not the cause of decline of one's physical, mental, and intellectual well-being. This line asks for social health, so that not just the teacher and student, but everyone around them, as well, live in harmony with each other, with their focus on a single pursuit: the quest for Self-knowledge.

Prayer		**Addresses**
saha nāvavatu	–	
saha nau bhunaktu	–	
saha vīryaṁ karvāvahai	–	
tejasvināvadhītamastu	–	
mā vidviṣāvahai	–	

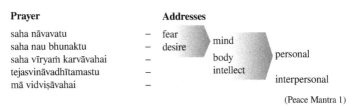

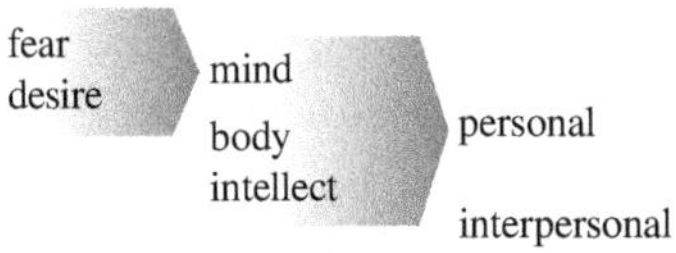

(Peace Mantra 1)

"Oṁ, peace, peace, peace."

Oṁ is the divine sound-vibration that permeates every atom of existence. Really speaking, Oṁ is the universe itself; that is, existence in the form of vibration.

There are three sources of disturbances in this universe: natural (*ādhidaivika*), physical (*ādhibhautika*), and metaphysical (*ādhyātmika*). The first source constitutes disturbances from nature, such as weather, natural calamities, and disasters. These are disturbances that are not in our control. The second source constitutes disturbances in our immediate surroundings, such as people and situations created by others. These are somewhat in our control but not completely, as everyone's actions and everything around us cannot be controlled. The third and last source of disturbance is the inner; that is, one's own mind. Even when the weather is pleasant and everything around us is in perfect harmony, we can be disturbed and distracted by an imagining of the future or a memory of the past. This source of disturbance is totally under our control if we have cultivated a certain level of self-mastery. This mantra asks the divine for peace from all three sources of disturbances.

Oṁ	divine sound-vibration	Sources of Disturbances
śāntiḥ	peace from natural	nature
śāntiḥ	peace from physical	others
śāntiḥ	peace from metaphysical	mind

Peace Mantra 2

ॐ आप्यायन्तु ममाङ्गानि वाक्प्राणश्चक्षुः श्रोत्रमथो बलमिन्द्रियाणि च सर्वाणि ।
सर्वं ब्रह्मौपनिषदं माऽहं ब्रह्म निराकुर्यां मा मा ब्रह्म निराकरोदनिराकरणमस्त्वनिराकरणं मेऽस्तु तदात्मनि निरते य उपनिषत्सु धर्मास्ते मयि सन्तु ते मयि सन्तु ॥
ॐ शान्तिः शान्तिः शान्तिः

oṁ āpyāyantu mamāṅgāni vākprāṇaścakṣuḥ śrotramatho balamindriyāṇi ca sarvāṇi,
sarvaṁ brahmaupaniṣadaṁ mā'haṁ brahma nirākuryāṁ mā mā brahma nirākarodanirākaraṇamastvanirākaraṇaṁ me'stu tadātmani nirate ya upaniṣatsu dharmāste mayi santu te mayi santu.
oṁ śāntiḥ śāntiḥ śāntiḥ

Translation:
Oṁ. May my limbs, speech, breath, eyes, and ears, and the function of all my senses become vitalized (so I may realize that) all is Brahman (the divine, supreme principle) of the *Upaniṣads*. May I never disconnect from Brahman, nor Brahman ever disconnect from me. May there be no denial (of that Brahman), absolutely none in me. May all the virtues sung in the *Upaniṣads* live in me, who am devoted to (the inquiry of) my true nature. May they all reside in me!
Oṁ, peace, peace, peace.

THIS IS another beautiful prayer in which the student asks the divine for strength of the body, mind, and intellect. The strength asked for is not for beauty, fame, success, or pleasure, but for knowledge. Any knowledge, including the ultimate knowledge that will be explored here, can only be acquired and practiced if the body, mind, and intellect are in sound condition. The student prays for health and fitness not as a goal unto itself, but as a means to enable a direct experience of the ultimate knowledge that the entire world is nothing but a manifestation of Brahman (the divine, supreme principle).

The student prays for not just a fleeting experience of Brahman, but a constant union with it. This union is termed *yoga*. As in any relationship, it has to be a two-way connection for it to yield its fullest benefit. The individual and the divine both have to remain connected to each other. The divine is always available, but the person will not experience the divine until and unless he makes a connection with that ultimate principle. A person could be living by the banks of a river, but to quench his thirst, he has to go to the river and drink the water himself; the same applies with the individual and the divine. The most important quality required in a student for this is unquestionable faith (*śraddhā*), which is what is meant by "non-denial" in the mantra.

The poem ends with the student pouring forth a heartfelt prayer to the divine to fill him with noble virtues. The student is not approaching the *Upaniṣad* just for intellectual stimulation, but wants to imbibe the knowledge contained therein. He wants to cultivate the noble qualities that will make his life fulfilled, and in turn, the lives of those around him. The student's repeat of this last plea twice further reveals his sincerity. He wants to embody the teaching of the *Upaniṣad*. He wants to know his true nature (*ātman*). He wants to become a living *Upaniṣad*. The embodiment of the teachings by individuals is what keeps a tradition alive.

The student is essentially praying for an inner revolution, which Baba Muktananda, the world-renowned Guru of the twentieth century, termed a "meditation revolution." This is an inside-outside revolution, where the purpose is not to change anyone or anything, but to change oneself; not to change the world, but to change one's vision; not to change things on the outside, but to change one's thoughts on the inside. It is this revolution alone that can bring about peace in the individual, and hence out in the world. This is the real solution to cure the violence we see in the world today.

Revolution (outside)	**Meditation Revolution (inside)**
change someone/something	change oneself
change the world	change one's vision
change things	change one's thoughts
	↓
	peace inside
	↓
	peace outside

CHAPTER ONE

The Question

"By what power does the mind think?"

In this chapter, the student asks a profound question, and the teacher gives a pointer that not only answers the question but also gives the student a powerful firsthand experience of the truth of it.

Verse 1

ॐ केनेषितं पतति प्रेषितं मनः
केन प्राणः प्रथमः प्रैति युक्तः ।
केनेषितां वाचमिमां वदन्ति
चक्षुः श्रोत्रं क उ देवो युनक्ति ॥ १ ॥

(1) oṁ keneṣitaṁ patati preṣitaṁ manaḥ
kena prāṇaḥ prathamaḥ praiti yuktaḥ,
keneṣitāṁ vācamimāṁ vadanti
cakṣuḥ śrotraṁ ka u devo yunakti.

Translation:
(Student:) Oṁ. Enlivened and inspired by what (power) (or by whom) does the mind jump (from one thought to next)? By what (power) does the first breath emerge to function? Enlivened by what (power) are these words spoken? What divine light directs the eye (to see) and the ear (to hear)?

THE *KENA UPANIṢAD* begins with the student asking his teacher a profound, reflective question in a straightforward manner. To ask such a question, a pause is a prerequisite. Especially in today's fast-paced and technologically advanced world, most run around so frantically in search of fulfillment that they have not a moment to take a break and reflect on the deeper purpose of their actions, let alone their thoughts. Busy striving to find happiness in people, things, and situations (in vain), most live convinced that pleasure, money, and fame are not only the benchmarks, but the source, of a fulfilled life. To exacerbate this plight, modern media, society, and sadly even education, do not challenge this assumption; worse, they reinforce it. The resultant stress, frustration, anxiety, and depression are not detected as red flags to this paradigm, either. The outcome is that hardly any ever get off the treadmill and deeply question the purpose of human life. The student here in the *Kena Upaniṣad* is one such highly mature individual. Fully convinced that searching for fulfillment outside is indeed a fruitless endeavor, leading to nothing but misery and its offshoots, he earnestly turns in a different direction: within. This transformation is evident in his question.

Interestingly, the name of neither the student nor the teacher is mentioned. Nothing about their background is mentioned, not even their gender or age. Is it possible that in his intense thirst for knowledge, the student forgot to mention his name or ask for the teacher's name? And is it possible that in his large-heartedness to share, the teacher never bothered to ask for the student's name or declare his own? The earnestness of the student must have been proof enough of the student's qualification and identity, and the powerful presence of the teacher must have been proof enough of the teacher's credibility and identity. Here we have a profound ancient text in which the author did not desire credit or acknowledgment. He chose to remain anonymous. Both the teacher and student knew that what was important was the knowledge—not the receiver, and not even the transmitter. It is the knowledge transmitted that is timeless and universal (sanātana).

The student's question is as follows: by what (kena) power (or by whom) does the mind think, the breath function, the speech work, the eye see, and the ear hear? The word *kena* can mean "by what?" or "by whom?" While the former translation is metaphysical (implying an impersonal divinity) in nature, the latter is theistic (implying a personal divinity), so the *Upaniṣad* leaves it up to the reader to choose which best suits his temperament.

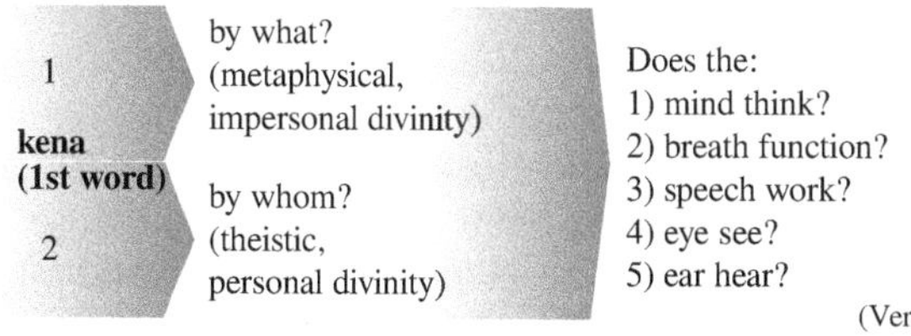

(Verse 1:1)

Regardless of the translation, the straightforwardness and sincerity of the student's question are beyond question. They reveal the clarity of his thought process, and in turn the maturity of his contemplation. The student is not asking out of intellectual curiosity, but out of a deep desire to understand the mystery of life. He is clear enough in his mind and articulate enough in his speech to consolidate into one simple five-fold question the numerous questions bugging the mind of any seeker.

The first question of the student is about the mind, undoubtedly the most essential subject of the entire yoga tradition. The mind thinks all day long, and even in sleep in the form of dreams. Mind is what enables us to function in this world. Upon contemplation, it is realized that each individual views the world through the lens of his mind, so each individual really lives in his own world. Notions of like or dislike, friend or enemy, fortune or misfortune, pleasant or unpleasant, favorable or unfavorable, credit or blame, happiness or sadness, and so on are mere thoughts, not objective or permanent. Even the concepts of "mine" and "not mine" are ultimately nothing but thoughts. For instance, the notion "my car" is a mere thought in my mind because the car does not claim that it belongs to me, and the notion "my friend" is a simply a thought because that person is a stranger to many, and could even be disliked by some. Thus, all notions are subjective and also temporary. They are provisional, no doubt useful for daily functioning, but not real in the ultimate sense. Taking them to be real is the source of much agitation. Most of us are in this predicament; we are caught in the content of our minds, so the desires and fears of our minds drive our lives.

The subject of the mind has fascinated humans since the dawn of civilization, and Western philosophy and psychology study the mind extensively. Whereas Western philosophy tries to gain a conceptual understanding of the mind, Western psychology tries to understand how the mind affects behavior. Yoga, too, studies the mind; however, its purpose is drastically different, as echoed in the student's question here. Notice that the student is interested in neither an academic understanding of the mind nor its effect on behavior, but only in a direct understanding of the source of the mind. He wants to know the power because of which the mind is able to think, regardless of the subject matter of the mind.

Study of the Mind

Discipline	Purpose
1) Western philosophy	understand the mechanism of the mind in a conceptual way
2) Western psychology	understand how the mind affects behavior
3) Yoga	understand the source of the mind

In psychiatry, mental agitation (in extreme cases) may be diagnosed as a symptom of chemical imbalance in the brain; thus, the treatment prescribed may be medicine. In psychotherapy, agitation may be attributed to an unresolved past incident; therefore, the treatment may focus on understanding that incident. In the yoga tradition, the cause of agitation is identified as neither a chemical imbalance nor a past trauma, but as ignorance of understanding the source of the mind, so the technique offered is self-inquiry (ātma-vicāra); that is, a direct investigation into one's own being. The student here is mature enough to already have pinpointed that root cause of all misery.

Medicine might fix a problem or two, but it cannot cure all one's problems. A quick fix is at best only a temporary suppression that merely patches up the symptoms. Psychotherapy might resolve an issue, yet leave umpteen others unresolved. Self-inquiry, on the other hand, goes to the heart of the matter. It is clear that the student here has embraced this practice of self-inquiry.

Condition: Mental Agitation

Discipline	Approach	
	Cause	**Treatment**
Psychiatry	chemical imbalance	medicine
Psychotherapy	past trauma	therapy
Yoga	ignorance of the source of the mind	self-inquiry

The four questions that follow are simply an elaboration of this first question. By "first breath," what is meant is every single breath, not necessarily just the first breath post-conception; each inbreath is as critical as the first one. The five faculties mentioned (mind, breath, speech, eyes, and ears) collectively represent all the functions of the body. The functions that these faculties carry out—namely, thinking, breathing, speaking, seeing, and hearing—are all going on constantly within the body. This question reveals that the student already understands the body, mind, breath, and speech to be inert instruments animated by another entity altogether. A dead body cannot think, breathe, speak, see, or hear, which clearly points to the existence of an independent power enlivening the body. An apt example often used by modern teachers of Vedānta to explain this idea is that of electronic devices, which are nothing but instruments empowered by the electricity running through them. In other words, the question can be rephrased as follows: "Who thinks through the mind, who breathes through the breath, who speaks through speech, who sees through the eyes, who hears through the ears?"[5] It is the lack of this reflection that makes a person spend his entire lifetime taking himself to be nothing but a miserable person with a tragic biography, hopelessly seeking happiness outside, and consequently seeing others merely as competitors in an endless struggle for survival.

Meditation exercise

> Create a space for daily practice of meditation. To make it conducive for meditation, keep the space absolutely clean. Set up an altar, and place there a photo or a symbol you revere or are drawn toward for worship. Light a small lamp (of ghee or oil) and incense. Wave the lamp and incense, along with ringing a temple bell. Adopt a comfortable posture

[5] This is really a variation of the well-known practice of ātma-vicāra (self-inquiry), where the question asked is "Who am I?" Even though this method was mentioned in the ancient sacred texts of Vedānta, it was Ramana Maharshi, a great sage of the twentieth century, who first brought it to light in modern times.

on a meditation mat (or on a chair if the floor is not possible for you) and gently close your eyes. Instead of dwelling on the content of any thought that passes through your mind, ask yourself the following question: by whose power does the mind think? The body is inert matter. So, who thinks? Absorb yourself in this investigation.

A variation of this meditation technique is to focus on the breath. Since the body is inert matter, it cannot breathe by itself. Who infused the body with life force (breath)? Once the life force departs from the body, it cannot breathe, no matter how much anyone tries to resuscitate it. What power draws the breath in and pumps the breath out all day and night, even when the individual is fast asleep? So, who breathes? Absorb yourself in this investigation.

Verse 2

श्रोत्रस्य श्रोत्रं मनसो मनो यद्वाचो ह वाचं स उ प्राणस्य प्राणः ।
चक्षुषश्चक्षुरतिमुच्य धीराः प्रेत्यास्माल्लोकादमृता भवन्ति ॥ २ ॥

(2) śrotrasya śrotraṁ manaso mano yadvāco ha vācaṁ sa u prāṇasya prāṇaḥ,
cakṣuṣaścakṣuratimucya dhīrāḥ pretyāsmāllokādamṛtā bhavanti.

Translation:
(Teacher:) (That power) is the ear of the ear, the mind of the mind, the speech of speech, the breath of the breath, and the eye of the eye. By giving up (false identity rooted in the body, mind, and social status) and rising above this (dualistic experience of the) world, the wise become immortal (fearless).

THE TEACHER'S answer is an enigmatic and oft-quoted poetic verse. By more or less echoing the student's question, the teacher is suggesting that the answer is embedded in the question itself.

In our day-to-day language, we say, "I think, I breathe, I speak, I see, I hear." In that sense, "I" am the thinker, the breather, the speaker, the seer, and the hearer—all of it.

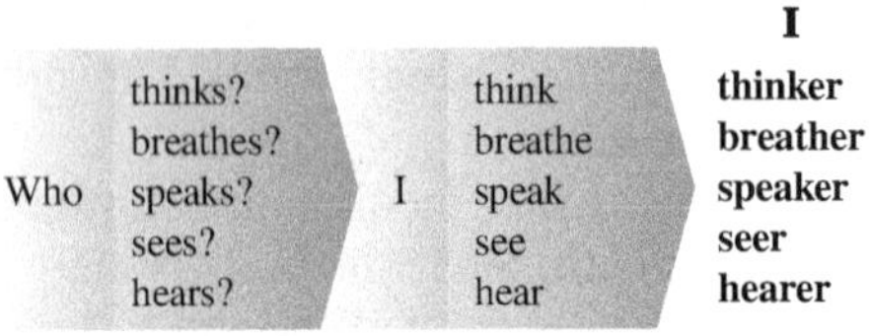

What is the nature of that "I"? Here the teacher explains, albeit in a cryptic way, that this I-Consciousness is separate from the mind, the breath, speech, and all the functions of the body. There is only one "I"—only one Consciousness—that functions through all the apparatuses of one's own body.

Not only that, there is only one "I" in all of existence. Everyone experiences "I think, I breathe, I speak, I see, I hear," which means the "I" in every being is one and the same; the differences lie in that with which the "I" identifies (namely, body and thoughts), not in the I-Consciousness itself.

Without "I," there would be no thought, no experience, no action, because there would be no one to think, experience, or act. Without "I," there would be no hearing through the ear, thinking through the mind, speaking through the speech, breathing through the breath, and seeing through the eye. Therefore, "I," or Consciousness is the essence—the ear of the ear, mind of the mind, speech of the speech, breath of the breath, and eye of the eye.

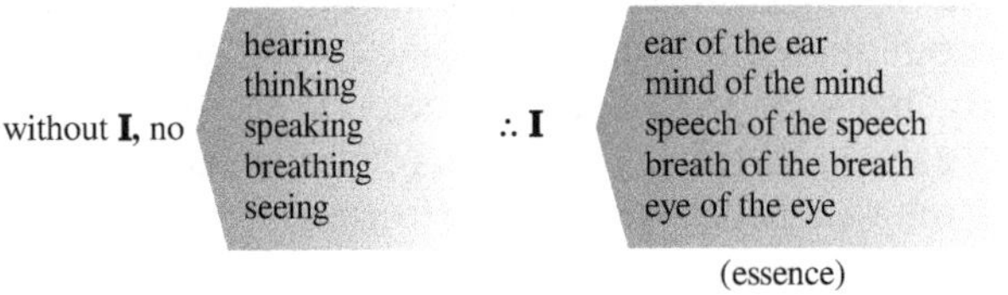

(Verse 1:2)

The clincher follows. Consciousness makes the body function, but is itself separate from the body, just as gas makes a car function, but is itself different from the car. The car depends on gas, not vice versa; it is the same with the body-mind and Consciousness. It is Consciousness that illumines and empowers all thoughts, experiences, and actions, but it exists independently of all thoughts, experiences, and actions. Without "I," no thoughts, experiences, or actions would take place, but the reverse is not true: "I exist" even in the absence of all thoughts, experiences, and actions.

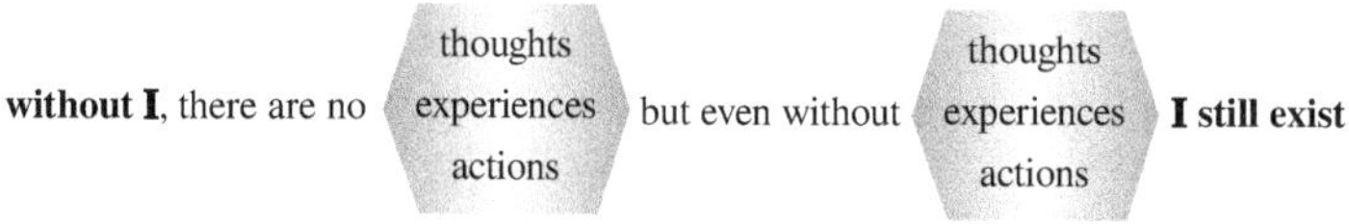

Wisdom lies in slowly distinguishing I-Consciousness from the body and the mind. In other words, wisdom is in understanding our identity to be separate from the conditioning put on us by society (social status), from our achievements, from the possessions we own, from the roles we play in our relationships, from the mental processes of our mind (personality), from our memories and goals, from our likes and dislikes, and even from the biological processes of our body (appearance, age, gender, and so on). Our identity is heavily determined by what others think of us and what our own mind thinks (mental conditioning). All these hitherto mentioned factors on which the individual bases his sense of selfhood are subject to change; in fact, they are constantly changing because that is the inescapable law of nature. The individual's identity is thus constantly under threat, challenged at every turn, by every change or even a possibility of a change. By depending on impermanent elements to maintain a sense of permanent identity and to experience permanent happiness, the individual becomes dependent on factors beyond his control. Consequently, the individual lives in a deep-seated fear and essentially spends his whole life safeguarding a fabricated identity.

Do I define myself based on:

- social status?
- achievements?
- possessions?
- relationships?
- personality?
- memories?
- goals?
- likes?
- dislikes?
- appearance?
- age?
- gender?

Given the unreality of this identity, it is not a surprise that it is fragile in nature and that constant defending of it is to no avail, for any little incident can burst its bubble. The constant struggle to maintain an identity and to become someone is itself the proof of its unreality. A real identity ought to be natural and not demand any effort toward its maintenance. The true Self is independent and needs no support to exist. It simply is: "I am." In this verse, the teacher is nudging the student to become free of all external crutches (status, possessions, relationships, appearance) and even of all internal crutches (thoughts and emotions), and learn to abide in that pure and independent I-Consciousness.

Meditation exercise

> How do you define yourself? Find a quiet spot, gently close your eyes, and contemplate this question. Think of all the external (status, possessions, relationships, appearance) and internal (thoughts and emotions) crutches you rely upon to create your sense of self. Contemplate the impermanent nature of all those factors. Try to find a sense of being within that is not dependent upon anything that is subject to change. When you begin to feel this sense of pure being, simply stay in that space for a few moments. Notice the inexplicable peace that arises with this recognition.

This practice of self-inquiry is a notch above the classic Western body-mind dualism, in which the mind is distinguished from the body, but Consciousness is not invoked in the equation at all.

The benefits of this practice for the disease of existential misery are stated right away in the verse: "Rising above this world" means gradually rising above a worldview rooted in the notions of "me" and "mine." As wisdom begins to arise, slowly a person becomes free of fear—the existential fear of death, and most importantly, its offshoot, the human insecurity over a lack of identity. Fear is what makes a person cling to things, people, and situations. Freedom from this fear is symbolically referred to in the verse as immortality (*amṛta*; *mṛta* means "death," so *amṛta* means "deathless"). The individual learns to let go and accept any outcome, as it is, without any complaints. Freedom from fear gives peace within and allows a person to radiate loving kindness on the outside.

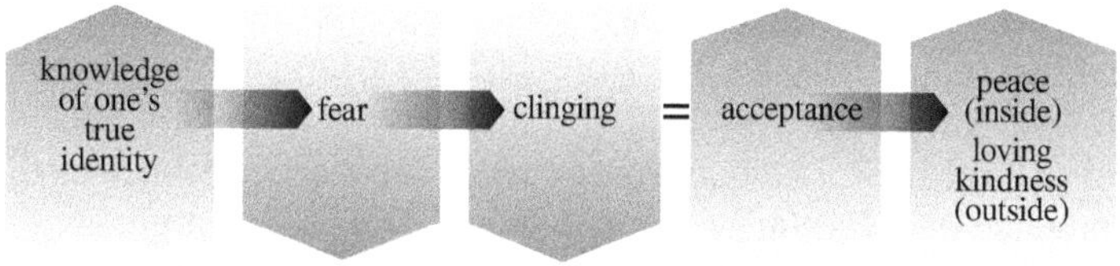

The parameters one uses to define oneself are the same that one uses to define others, so this practice has a direct impact on the quality of one's relationships. The individual begins to operate more and more out of selflessness, knowing that only one Consciousness exists in all the many forms. Such a being radiates loving kindness toward all. Fear and love are the opposites of each other, so it is but natural that the less fear exists within a person, the more loving kindness will radiate from him. This love need not necessarily be expressed in actions or words, for the very presence of a being is enough of an indicator to glean his inner state.

This verse conveyed the kernel of the teaching; the rest of the text is essentially an exposition of this teaching.

Verse 3

न तत्र चक्षुर्गच्छति न वाग्गच्छति नो मनो
न विद्मो न विजानीमो यथैतदनुशिष्यात् ।
अन्यदेव तद्विदितादथो अविदितादधि
इति शुश्रुम पूर्वेषां ये नस्तद्व्याचचक्षिरे ॥ ३ ॥

(3) na tatra cakṣurgacchati na vāggacchati no mano
na vidmo na vijānīmo yathaitadanuśiṣyāt,
anyadeva tadviditādatho aviditādadhi
iti śuśruma pūrveṣāṁ ye nastadvyācacakṣire.

Translation:
The eye does not go there, nor do speech or the mind. We do not know that (through the intellect; therefore,) we do not know how to teach (about it). That (Consciousness) is certainly other than the known, but it is definitely not unknown, either. Thus we have learned from our (lineage of) teachers, who gave us the knowledge of that (Consciousness).

IN THE FIRST two lines of this verse, the teacher delineates the practice of self-inquiry in a subtle way. The eye is arguably the most complex organ in the human body; in fact, some creationists have used its complexity as an argument against the theory of evolution. However, despite its extreme sophistication, the eye is incapable of seeing Consciousness. Language is a unique faculty of *Homo sapiens*, and many anthropologists believe the birth of human language to be the fountainhead of human culture. Many species can communicate via chemicals and vocalization, but language is uniquely human. It is the invisible currency for our daily functioning. However, when it comes to Consciousness, even language falls short. The human mind is more complex than that of any other species. This is reflected in the size of the human brain (in proportion to body size). Many species in the animal kingdom, such as dogs and elephants, exhibit emotions, but not to the extent that humans do. Even with such a refined mind, Consciousness lies beyond mental grasp.

The intellect is perhaps the most distinguishing feature of the human race. Some animals, such as chimpanzees (which can make simple tools) and dolphins, exhibit a high level of intelligence, but even they do not come close to having the degree of intelligence found in humans. The creation of culture is a product of human intellect alone. It is the intellect that allows humans to ask questions—to explore the outer world and the inner. It is the intellect that allowed humans to envision going to the moon, and eventually enabled them to reach the moon. But even this intellect cannot reach Consciousness.

Does that mean Consciousness is out of reach? Not at all. On the contrary, the verse implies that it is closer than the closest; in fact, it is so close that it is overlooked. The closer something is, the more difficult it is to see it; for example, one cannot see one's own eyes. Similarly, Consciousness is so close that it cannot be seen. It is subtler than—and closer than—the eyes, the breath, the speech, and even thoughts. It is beyond all names or words (*nāma*) and forms or objects (*rūpa*). It cannot be seen for it is the seer itself, that which sees. It does not need the help of any instrument—outer (microscope) or inner (the senses and mind)—to be known (for that would be indirect knowledge). Consciousness can only be realized directly as one's own being, as "I am." In this sense, it is the most obvious, undeniable fact of one's existence and requires no proof. To deny it is to actually affirm it. It is the only knowledge that can be classified as direct knowledge, because it requires no instrument, no intermediary, and no path.

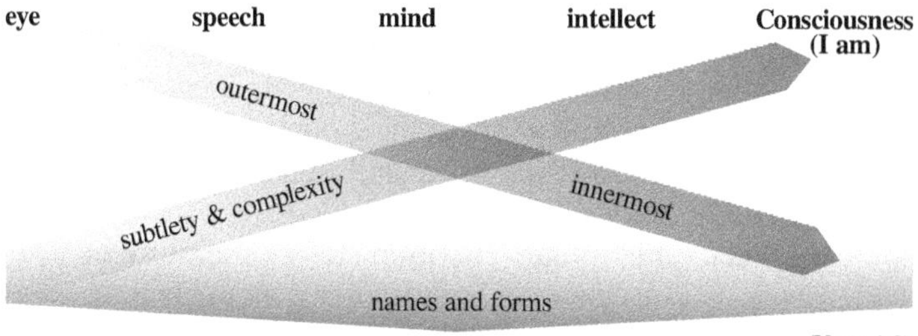

(Verse 1:3)

The teacher gives this knowledge directly because there is no process for teaching it, as it is not a thing that can be seen by the eyes, not a theme that can be discussed in words, not an idea that can be thought about by the mind, and not even a concept that can be imagined or reflected on by the intellect. It is just pure Awareness. In other words, "I exist" even bereft of my eyes (body), speech, thoughts, and insights. This is in total contrast with Western philosopher René Descartes' famous conclusion "Cogito ergo sum" ("I think, therefore I am"). According to the teacher here (and our own deep, honest, direct experience), "I am, whether I think or not."

René Descartes — I think, therefore I am.

***Kena Upaniṣad* — I am, whether I think or not.**

Meditation exercise

> Find a space of silence and solitude. Adopt a comfortable posture, with your spine straight and your neck in alignment with it. Become aware of your posture, and of your body. Scan the body from top to bottom, making sure all parts of the body are at ease, without any tension. If you find any tension in any part, bring your attention to that part and accept that, as well.
>
> Slowly turn your attention to the breath. Become aware of the breathing process—the inbreath and the outbreath—without forcing it in any way.
>
> After a few minutes of this, shift your attention to the mind. Become aware of the thoughts. Just watch them come and go, arise and subside, without pursuing or rejecting any.
>
> Then shift your attention to Consciousness itself—closer than the body, closer than the breath, closer than the thoughts. Become conscious of this pure Consciousness, and notice its nature: aware,

alive, empty, clear, timeless, and boundless. It is of the nature of peace that can never be disturbed. Stay in this spaceless space for some time, embracing it completely as your true nature.

In the second half of this verse, the teacher begins to explain further the reason this divine, supreme principle defies explanation. "It is other than the known": the known here refers to all knowledge, objective and subjective. Thus, knowledge includes the entire external world (people, objects, events) and the entire internal world (thoughts and emotions). The supreme principle is not an object; it is neither physical nor mental, neither visible nor invisible. If it were, it would be limited in space and time, and thus not the supreme principle enlivening all objects and thoughts.

If the supreme principle is not the known, then by definition, it would be the unknown. But the teacher immediately follows up by clarifying that it is beyond the unknown. Therefore, it is neither the known nor the unknown. This defies binary logic. How can something be neither this nor not this? After stating that the supreme principle is not an object of knowledge, the teacher must have immediately realized that the student could misunderstand it to be distant, foreign, beyond reach. That is not the case at all. It is not an object of knowledge, but that does not mean it is not knowable. The only way we can reconcile these two statements—namely, that it is both not known and not unknown—is by concluding that the supreme principle is knowledge, or Consciousness, itself. In that space of pure knowledge, the triad of knower (individual), known (object), and knowing (process) vanish.

Statement 1: It is not known.

Statement 2: But it is not unknown. (Verse 1:3)

Conclusion: ∴ It is knowledge (Consciousness) itself.

In the Vedic tradition, there are four primary means of proof (*pramāṇa*): the words of scripture, personal experience, bona fide teachers, and logic. Thus far, the teacher has explained this subtle subject using crystal clear logic and the conviction of his own direct experience. To stamp it as a timeless and universal truth (sanātana), and not just some eccentric logic or experience, he invokes the lineage of teachers to which he belongs. Vedic knowledge was transmitted orally and was written down only much later; regardless of the method of teaching, the teacher-student relationship is at the heart of the tradition. This knowledge has been passed down from teacher to student since time immemorial. It has stood the test of time. By sincerely following the practices given by the teachers, any student can have the experience to which they have pointed. No one can claim an exclusive right—a copyright or trademark—to this ultimate knowledge. It reveals the teacher's humility, for he does not claim to have come up with a new teaching or a new tradition. He openly owes his own enlightened state to the teachings and the grace of his teacher, who received it from his teacher, and so on. The remembrance of his lineage reveals the gratitude each teacher feels for his teacher and the entire lineage for imparting the teachings and the experience that transformed his life, and in turn, that of others.

Verse 4

यद्वाचाऽनभ्युदितं येन वागभ्युद्यते ।
तदेव ब्रह्म त्वं विद्धि नेदं यदिदमुपासते ॥ ४ ॥

(4) yadvācā'nabhyuditaṁ yena vāgabhyudyate,
tadeva brahma tvaṁ viddhi nedaṁ yadidamupāsate.

Translation:
That which speech cannot describe but because of which speech functions, that alone is Brahman (the divine, supreme principle), not that which people worship (in different names).

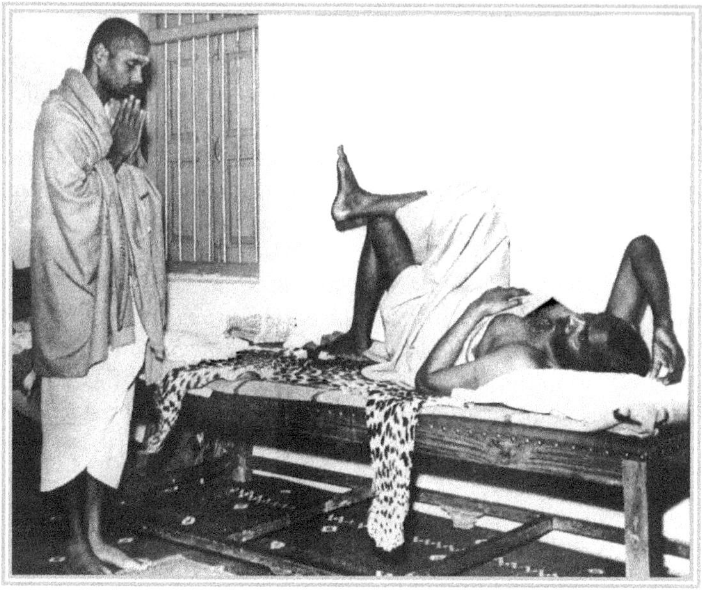

Baba Muktananda with his Guru, Bhagavan Nityananda,
in the village of Ganeshpuri in Maharashtra, India

Photo: M. D. Suvarna, Foto Corner

IN THE PREVIOUS verse, the teacher admitted that the divine, supreme principle, the source of all life, is so subtle and so close to one's being that it is not an object that can be given or taken in a transaction, and not even an idea that can be exchanged in words. Even though making this limitation clear at the outset can seem disheartening to the student, it is stated to raise the spirits of the student in two ways: first, to show that the supreme principle is one's own being, so close it cannot even be pointed to, and second, that this principle cannot be taught in words, but a true master has the ability to give a direct experience of it to a sincere student. Baba Muktananda, one such great master, traveled throughout the world in 1970s and early 1980s awakening thousands by giving them a firsthand experience of the divine within. This transmission[6] is at the heart of the Guru-disciple relationship. Just as Śrī Kṛṣṇa gave Arjuna a direct experience of God in chapter 11 of the *Bhagavad Gītā (The Song of God)*, so in the remaining verses of this chapter, the teacher begins to sing the glory of Brahman in order to plunge the student into the experience of oneness with that divinity as pure Consciousness.

The teacher begins by pointing out our inadequacy when it comes to giving the divine a name. Religious and spiritual traditions across the world and across the ages have given many names to the divine: God, Allah, Yahweh, Christ, Buddha, Kṛṣṇa, Śiva, Rāma, and so on. In the Hindu tradition, there are chants that list as many as a thousand names of a particular deity, such as the *Viṣṇu Sahasranāma* (*The Thousand Names of Viṣṇu*), *Śiva Sahasranāma* (*The Thousand Names of Śiva*), and *Lalitā Sahasranāma* (*The Thousand Names of Lalitā*). Many religions, especially the Abrahamic faiths, have conflicts over which is the true God or the supreme God. Here, the teacher points out that Brahman, the divine, supreme principle, cannot be captured in any name. It is beyond names because words belong to the realm of objects and thoughts, and the supreme principle is the source of all objects and all thoughts. Note that this is not to dismiss

[6] This transmission is known as *śaktipāta* in the ancient tradition of Kashmir Shaivism, whose teachings Baba Muktananda brought to the West in the 1970s.

the practice of worshipping the divine by name; it is simply a warning not to create a conflict with others who use a different name for their worship.

Furthermore, in the human body, the tongue is able to speak only if there is life force present in the body. The entire mechanism of speech production in the body is highly complex, but the moment the life force departs from the body, no word can be uttered. This shows that the source, namely Consciousness, that gives life to the body and makes speech function is much greater than speech itself, for the latter is dependent on the former, and not the other way around. Speech is simply an expression of Consciousness, so how can a part of the whole describe or capture the whole?

Besides its profound metaphysical implications, this verse also has a very pragmatic application. If all words are finite and incomplete, and if the supreme principle is infinite and complete, then all conversations—whether spiritual or material, religious or secular—are incomplete and can never capture the complete truth. All expositions are simply different viewpoints that capture part of reality and never the whole of it. This is beautifully illustrated in the famous ancient Indian story of the blind men and the elephant, in which each person touches a different part of the elephant and comes to a different conclusion about what it is, based on his limited experience. While each might be valid from his perspective, no one has the complete truth. Collaboration can help them identify the object as an elephant, but that requires each to accept the limitations of his subjective experience. This understanding will make us less assertive in expressing our viewpoints and allow us to let others express their viewpoints more freely, without feeling compelled to agree or disagree. In light of this understanding, conversations and dialogues are useful, but all arguments are useless. We place so much value on praise and criticism, but when we understand words in the manner described here, we stop taking to heart praise and criticism and no longer let them affect our self-esteem.

Most importantly, this verse points out the futility of words in communicating the supreme principle. While words are important and necessary for daily functioning, silence alone is of value when it comes to connecting with the divine, finding the complete truth, and experiencing eternal peace.

Meditation exercise

> Find a spot either out in nature or in a park, in your workplace, or even in a shopping mall. Sit there by yourself, in silence, and just listen. Listen to the sound of nature or the noise of the marketplace. Your eyes can either be closed or left open. The key here is to simply listen and resist the urge to judge or speak anything. Understand that all sounds and all words are fragmentations, and hence not capable of conveying the complete truth. There is no reason to accept or reject, endorse or oppose, any viewpoint. There is also equally no reason to express (or even have) any viewpoint. Enjoy the silence of the tongue, and ultimately, of the mind, as it begins to have fewer and fewer thoughts.

Verse 5

यन्मनसा न मनुते येनाहुर्मनो मतम् ।
तदेव ब्रह्म त्वं विद्धि नेदं यदिदमुपासते ॥ ५ ॥

(5) yanmanasā na manute yenāhurmano matam,
tadeva brahma tvaṁ viddhi nedaṁ yadidamupāsate.

Translation:
That which the mind cannot think about but because of which the mind thinks, that alone is Brahman, not that which people worship (in their imagination).

NOW THE TEACHER proceeds to explain the inability of the mind to imagine the supreme principle. Again, a part of the whole cannot capture the whole. It is Consciousness that enables the mind to think, so the latter is only a part of the former. Think of a wave in the ocean: the ocean is the cause, the wave an effect. Similarly, the mind is simply a wave, as it were, in the ocean of Consciousness. Given this, how can the mind fathom its cause?

The different descriptions of the divine within different faiths are simply different ways of the mind to imagine the unimaginable. There are as many ways to describe worship as there are worshippers. Each imagination of the divine is valid for the worshipper. While each description is complete for that worshipper, it is not complete enough to provide him the license to impose it on anyone else. Nowhere else is this idea reflected better in practice than in the religious harmony seen within India, where at least 330 million gods and goddesses and countless descriptions of the divine are worshipped simultaneously. The unstated, underlying understanding is that while "my god is perfect for me, your god is perfect for you;" in the end, all gods are nothing but our minds trying to put a frame around the limitless. Since the divine is infinite, there are infinite ways to worship that divine.

This verse also has implications for our relationships. Often we find ourselves brooding over and acting according to what others think of us. The way other people see us often defines our self-image. This can have major ramifications, the most important being that we outsource the determinant of our self-esteem, a habit that can be very debilitating, to say the least. This verse points out the limitations of our personal vision, because the supreme principle, or the ultimate truth, cannot be thought about or boxed into any mental construct. Thus, the verse implies that any opinion we hold is limited and not the complete truth. While someone's opinion of us can reveal a blind spot within our personality, it is wise to take such opinions with a grain of salt because they have been filtered through a limited mind; most importantly, they cannot capture the limitless supreme principle, which is our true nature. A wise person uses the opinions of others to enhance his understanding of his true identity, not hamper it. Ultimately, whatever anyone thinks of us—or even what we think of ourselves—is not who we truly are; as this verse points out, our true nature is beyond thought.

The next verse further elaborates on this idea.

Meditation exercise

> Sit still and gently close your eyes. Know that whatever others think of you and whatever your mind thinks of yourself are nothing more than a fabrication of the mind. It is not who you truly are. Your biography is simply a story compiled by stringing together a series of thoughts. Abide in the peace of knowing that your true identity is beyond all thoughts of yourself and of others. Feel in your own heart: "I have no biography. I am not what anyone thinks of me. I am not what I think."

Verse 6

यच्चक्षुषा न पश्यति येन चक्षूंषि पश्यति ।
तदेव ब्रह्म त्वं विद्धि नेदं यदिदमुपासते ॥ ६ ॥

(6) yaccakṣuṣā na paśyati yena cakṣūṁṣi paśyati,
tadeva brahma tvaṁ viddhi nedaṁ yadidamupāsate.

Translation:
That which the eye cannot see but because of which the eye sees, that alone is Brahman, not that which people worship (in various forms: symbols, icons, statues).

THE TRADITION of Vedānta explains that names (nāma) and forms (rūpa) are interlinked: each name has a form, and each form has a name. When it comes to our experience of the world, the two cannot exist without each other. This verse continues to drive home the point stated in the previous two verses that all knowledge (mental) and all experience (sensory) are limited and are not the complete truth or the supreme principle. Every form we experience with our senses is nothing but a thought in the mind, as it is seen in the mind. Since the mind is limited by its nature, everything the mind can think of is equally limited. Thus, every form is incomplete, incapable of capturing the supreme principle, which is infinite. This explains the nearly countless forms of the divine envisioned in the Hindu tradition. The range is incredible, to the extent that one and the same deity (Śiva) is worshipped both as an inert stone (Śiva *liṅga*) and as a not only fully alive but as an androgynous being (*ardhanārīśvara*). The wise realized that "while my beloved might be the most beautiful for me, it doesn't have to be so for everyone." There is no reason to impose one's own form of the divine on someone else. Each form is best suited for the worshipper of that form.

Meditation exercise

> Gently close your eyes and mentally invoke the form of the divine you worship or you find yourself drawn toward. Eliminate all other thoughts from your mind and just focus on this one form. Understand that form to be a gateway to the divine, supreme principle. Understand that while the form may be finite, the principle it represents is infinite. That form is nothing but an embodiment of the divine. Reflecting thus, absorb yourself in that form. Forget your own form and story, and lose yourself in the form and the story of the divine as you envision it.

Verse 7

यच्छ्रोत्रेण न शृणोति येन श्रोत्रमिदꣳश्रुतम् ।
तदेव ब्रह्म त्वं विद्धि नेदं यदिदमुपासते ॥ ७ ॥

(7) yacchrotreṇa na śṛṇoti yena śrotramidaṁśrutam,
tadeva brahma tvaṁ viddhi nedaṁ yadidamupāsate.

Translation:
That which the ear cannot hear (about) but because of which the ear hears, that alone is Brahman, not that which people worship (by various devotional chants).

CONTINUING THE SAME line of thought, the teacher sings that no devotional chant or song of any religious tradition can fully capture the glory of the divine. No matter how melodious and how profound a chant may be, it cannot fully convey the power of the divine because the supreme principle is the source and the power that allow the ear to hear the chant. Again, this is not to dismiss the practice of chanting; it just makes one aware that hearing also only takes place because of the existence of Consciousness.

Verse 8

यत्प्राणेन न प्राणिति येन प्राणः प्रणीयते ।
तदेव ब्रह्म त्वं विद्धि नेदं यदिदमुपासते ॥ ८ ॥

(8) yatprāṇena na prāṇiti yena prāṇaḥ praṇīyate,
tadeva brahma tvaṁ viddhi nedaṁ yadidamupāsate.

Translation:
That which the breath (or life force) cannot enliven but because of which the breath (or life force) enlivens (all forms), that alone is Brahman, not that which people worship (by various rituals and activities).

IN THE LAST verse of this chapter, the teacher sums it all up by stating in unequivocal terms that all activity takes place due to the divine, supreme principle, which is pure Consciousness. All forms are inert unless powered by that supreme principle. That

Limited		Unlimited
names & forms	speech (Verse 1:4) mind (Verse 1:5) eyes (Verse 1:6) ears (Verse 1:7) breath (Verse 1:8)	Consciousness

alone is Brahman, which is itself nameless and formless, but is the source of and the power behind all names and forms. That Brahman is none other than pure Consciousness, one's own being. To even understand this, let alone realize it, requires an extremely subtle intellect.

॥ इति प्रथमः खण्डः ॥

iti prathamaḥ khaṇḍaḥ.

Thus ends chapter one.

CHAPTER TWO

The Test

"Do you know that power?"

In this chapter, the teacher tests the depth of the disciple's understanding. The teacher also gives a subtle technique to instantly transform a mundane life into a life divine.

Verse 1

यदि मन्यसे सुवेदेति दहरमेवापि नूनम् । त्वं वेत्थ ब्रह्मणो रूपं
यदस्य त्वं यदस्य देवेष्वथ नु मीमाꣳस्यमेव ते मन्ये विदितम् ॥ १ ॥

(1) yadi manyase suvedeti daharamevāpi nūnam, tvaṁ vettha brahmaṇo rupaṁ
yadasya tvaṁ yadasya deveṣvatha nu mīmāṁsyameva te manye viditam.

Translation:
(Teacher:) If you think you know it well, then truly you have understood very little. The divine nature of Brahman is still not completely known by you. Therefore, I believe you have to inquire further into the nature of Brahman.

AFTER SINGING the glory of one's true nature as pure Consciousness, the teacher here sets out to test the disciple's understanding. The teacher must have seen the glow on the disciple's face as his entire being was lit up by the realization of his true nature. The grace of the divine or the Guru can give an open-minded seeker an instant experience of his divine nature. In an enlightened master's presence, this sublime experience can come quite naturally, albeit in different degrees, depending on the maturity of the seeker. However, to remain established in the highest state usually takes a long time because the seeker's mental conditioning needs to be undone. Here, the power of the teacher's words and presence must have been sufficient to catapult the disciple into a nondual awareness of Consciousness. To ensure his stability in that state, the teacher puts forth a question to the disciple, essentially asking him, "Do you know that Consciousness?"

The student is now in a fix. The teacher has already explained that Consciousness is not an object of knowledge. At the same time, if the student answers that he does not know Consciousness, then he is admitting his ignorance of a truth that was explained by the teacher as the most obvious fact of existence. The teacher challenges the disciple so the latter may reveal his state.

Verse 2

नाहं मन्ये सुवेदेति नो न वेदेति वेद च ।
यो नस्तद्वेद तद्वेद नो न वेदेति वेद च ॥ २ ॥

(2) nāhaṁ manye suvedeti no na vedeti veda ca,
yo nastadveda tadveda no na vedeti veda ca.

Translation:
(Student:) I do not know it well. It is not that I do not know it; I know it. He among us who knows that (Brahman), knows that it is both known and unknown.

GIVEN THE NATURE of the question, the student's reply is in paradoxical language. The student first denies his knowledge of Consciousness, then negates his ignorance of it, and then finally admits his complete knowledge of it. It might seem the student is trying to cover all possibilities in an intellectual manner; however, that could not be further from the truth. Each reply of the student is pregnant with meaning, and it is incumbent upon us to decode each word spoken by the student to understand the depth of realization underlying it.

The student basically gives three answers:

(1) I do not know Consciousness well.
Consciousness cannot be known as a thing or a thought. Everything is experienced by the senses and known by the mind because of the light of Consciousness. Without Consciousness, there would be no experience and no knowledge, no object and no thought. Consciousness is the knower, and the world (both outer and inner) is the known. To reduce Consciousness to an object of knowledge is, in fact, at the root of one's mistaken identity steeped in the body, mind, and social status.

(2) It is not that I do not know Consciousness.
The student quickly realizes that his statement "I do not know

it" can be taken literally to mean he did not understand or experience the teaching imparted. In this statement, we see an attempt by the student to clarify that this is not what he meant by his earlier claim.

(3) I know Consciousness very well.

Finally, the student cannot resist admitting his direct experience. The student knows Consciousness as his own Self, the awareness "I am." It is the most—and the only—direct knowledge because all other knowledge is known through the instruments of the mind and the senses. One's knowledge of one's existence is beyond doubt and cannot be denied or negated. In this statement, the student articulates his conviction that "I know Consciousness not as an object but as the very subject." In other words, the student is exclaiming his realization: "I am Consciousness." Consciousness is the source, substance, and end of all there is. All that is known is Consciousness alone, for nothing exists outside the light of Consciousness. Consciousness alone exists. All there is is awareness of the Self: I am, I am.

Knowing fully well that his language defies logic and could sound like the rambling of a madman, the student declares that only those who have recognized the Self as pure Consciousness, one with all of existence, would understand the profound import behind his answer. Consciousness is prior to and beyond language; therefore, it cannot be explained in words. The student has nonetheless tried his level best. Those who have not had the experience of pure Consciousness will not understand the student's answer, but those who have will understand it. It is a matter of firsthand experience, not intellectual understanding, logical analysis, or academic study.

Verse 3

यस्यामतं तस्य मतं मतं यस्य न वेद सः ।
अविज्ञातं विजानतां विज्ञातमविजानताम् ॥ ३ ॥

(3) yasyāmataṁ tasya mataṁ mataṁ yasya na veda saḥ,
avijñātaṁ vijānatāṁ vijñātamavijānatām.

Translation:
(Teacher:) He knows who knows that he cannot know it (Consciousness); he knows not who thinks he knows. It is unknown to those who claim to be knowers; it is known to those who do not claim to be knowers.

HEARING THE STUDENT'S brilliant reply, filled with the potency of his Self-knowledge, the teacher confirms the student's enlightened state of being. In this verse, the teacher elaborates on the student's reply for the sake of the other seekers sitting around them and also to celebrate the disciple's liberation from the bondage of a mistaken identity.

To claim, "I know X" automatically implies that X is different from me: I am the knower, and X is an object of knowledge. Consciousness is one's own Self, not a thing that can be known as separate from "I," the knower. Any object of knowledge is simply a thought (information) in the mind, but Consciousness is the very source and substratum of the mind.

Meditation exercise

> Gently close your eyes and reflect on everything that is in your field of awareness. This would include any external object of knowledge (person, thing, situation) and any internal object of knowledge (emotion, thought). If it is an object of knowledge, then it can be classified as the "known." Ask yourself, "Who is the knower of all that is known?" When you say, "I know," who is that "I" who knows?

> What is the nature of that "I"? Absorb yourself in this investigation.

Furthermore, when the true nature of one's Self is clearly recognized as pure Consciousness, the world is seen as an expression of that Consciousness. He who has recognized his own Self as pure Consciousness will, therefore, never fall into the delusion of claiming some sort of special knowledge that makes him feel superior to others. In fact, Self-knowledge is the dissolution of precisely this arrogance of the individual identity (*ahaṁkāra*) that thinks and wants to show "I know more than you do," "I am better than you," "I am superior to you," or even "I am more spiritual, purer than you." A truly awakened being does not see anyone as different from his own Self.

Even when read in a different way, this verse has a profound implication; namely, that no one can claim complete knowledge of life. The mind is limited, and the world—which is a reflection of infinite Consciousness—is infinite. There are infinite names and forms. How can the finite (individual) ever know the infinite (divine)? In any scientific analysis, a conclusion is drawn based on the data points acquired. Who has acquired all the data points of life? Everything is constantly in flux, so who knows it all, really? Only nature (divine) knows, for nature has an inbuilt memory known as *karma*. Everything happens according to this natural law of karma, the action-reaction principle. Each individual harvests the fruits of the seeds he has sown, whether knowingly or unknowingly, whether he remembers it or not, whether in this or in a past lifetime. Moreover, no one can precisely predict the outcome (fruits) of his actions (seeds), as there are several forces at work that lie out of his hands.[7] No individual has all the knowledge to pronounce a judgement on any situation or any person. In the light of this, no situation is favorable or unfavorable; no one is innocent and no one is guilty; and there is no one to give credit to and no one to blame for the situation in which one finds oneself.

[7] This principle is explained in the *Bhagavad Gītā*, 2.47.

Meditation exercise

> With eyes open or closed, reflect thus on the current situation in your life: Think of the countless events, major or (seemingly) minor, that contributed to the making of your present moment. Did you have the power to direct all the factors that resulted in your present situation? Had you predicted the present outcome of your past actions? Do you know how your present actions will result in the unfolding of your future destiny? Contemplate how little you know or have control over in this endless flow of life. Given this, fully accept your present situation, whatever it may be, without labeling it as favorable or unfavorable.

In the second half of this verse, the teacher repeats the same idea to emphasize his point. A wise person knows that because the nature of Consciousness is silence, its true nature cannot be communicated in words. Words are only pointers to guide us to that ultimate knowledge, which is beyond words. Silence is the source from which all words emerge and into which they all dissolve back.

Verse 4

प्रतिबोधविदितं मतममृतत्वं हि विन्दते ।
आत्मना विन्दते वीर्यं विद्यया विन्दतेऽमृतम् ॥ ४ ॥

(4) pratibodhaviditaṁ matamamṛtatvaṁ hi vindate,
ātmanā vindate vīryaṁ vidyayā vindate'mṛtam.

Translation:
Truly, he attains immortality who is aware (of Consciousness) in every experience (or in every thought or every state of consciousness). Through self-effort, inner strength is attained. Through Self-knowledge, immortality (fearlessness) is attained.

AT THIS JUNCTURE, the teacher provides a subtle technique students can practice even while performing their daily activities, for all who need one. Every experience of the senses and the mind (*pratibodha*) takes place only because of the light of Consciousness. There has to be an experiencer for any experience to take place. That experiencer is I-Consciousness. For this reason, all experiences and all thoughts only prove the existence of Consciousness, without which they would not exist. They borrow their existence from Consciousness.

Normally, we get lost in the content of an experience or a thought. Depending on our likes and dislikes, we pursue certain objects of sight, sound, smell, taste, and touch, and avoid others. To get everything we like and manage to avoid everything we do not is just impossible. To believe otherwise only creates anger and frustration. Here the teacher suggests the following alternative: instead of getting enchanted by the content of the experience, whether external or internal, become enchanted by the experiencer, Consciousness, in whose light the experience is taking place. That Consciousness itself remains pure and totally unaffected by the nature of any experience or the content of any thought.

Furthermore, since our experience of objects outside and thoughts inside is known only because we are conscious of them, all experience is made up only of Consciousness. The substance out of which every experience and thought is composed, no matter its nature or content, is nothing other than Consciousness. The metaphor often used in nondual traditions is that of waves and water: all waves are of different size and shape, but all are made up of the same substance, namely water; similarly, all things in manifestation are different in name and form but made up of the same substance, namely Consciousness.

In this way, every experience, every thought, becomes an opportunity to recognize our true nature. If this vision is cultivated, every experience, whether pleasant or unpleasant, is a mirror to behold our real identity. This approach to life begins to take away any fear through which we may engage with the world, explained here by promising the nectar of immortality (amṛta) as the fruit of this practice. This shift in awareness is a subtle form of self-effort. When the seeker carries out his life with this awareness, the benefits are immense. The foremost benefit is inner strength (vīryam). This means he is no longer dependent on the world to give him security.

Meditation exercise

> As you carry out your daily activities, become aware of how the senses receive sensory input from the outer world: the eyes see forms, the ear hears sounds, and so on. Also, become aware of the thoughts that pass through your inner world. Contemplate that, without Consciousness, no experience would be possible, neither outer nor inner. In this manner, instead of getting lost in the content of the perception (of objects) and cognition (of thoughts), turn your attention toward the light of this Consciousness, because of which and in which all perceptions and cognitions take place. No matter what you hear, touch, see, taste, smell, or think, keep your attention on the light of Consciousness, the space in which all experiences transpire. Nothing can ever sully that Consciousness.
>
> A variation of this meditation technique is as follows. Contemplate that because, without Consciousness, there would be no perception or cognition, the substance out of which every perception and cognition is made up is nothing but Consciousness. No matter what happens around you and no matter what thoughts arise inside you, accept it, without pursuing or fighting it, as just another form of Consciousness. Whether you are sitting still or going about performing your daily tasks, cultivate the following awareness: "Everything I experience is my own Consciousness. There is nothing outside of that Consciousness. The distinction of outside and inside are with reference to the body, not to Consciousness. There is nothing other than the experience of 'I am.'"

Pratibodha can also be understood as "every state of consciousness." Every human being naturally experiences three states of consciousness: the waking state, the dream state, and the dreamless sleep (or deep sleep) state. The waking state is composed of objects, thoughts, and the veil that conceals Self-knowledge (*māyā*); the dream state is composed of thoughts and ignorance; and the deep sleep state is composed of just the veil of ignorance, experienced as darkness.

State	Composed of		
waking	objects	thoughts	ignorance
dream	—	thoughts	ignorance
deep sleep	—	—	ignorance

In the waking state, the awake person interacts with the waking world; in the dream state, the dreamer interacts with the dream world; and in the deep sleep state, both the person and the corresponding world disappear into oblivion. In waking state, the person feels, "I am awake"; upon waking up from a dream, the person feels, "I had a dream"; and upon waking up from deep sleep, the person feels, "I had no dreams. I slept well." This clearly shows that the sense of "I," or the light of Consciousness, runs throughout all three states.[8] It is ever-present; truly speaking, it is beyond the dimension of time—always right now, right here.

State	Experience
waking	I am awake
dream	I had a dream
deep sleep	I had no dreams

common factor: **I**

[8] This topic is explored in several sacred texts of the nondual traditions of Advaita Vedānta and Kashmir Shaivism.

This light of Consciousness illumines every state and the appearance and disappearance of each of them, itself remaining apart from all of them. The awake person and the waking world, the dreamer and the dream world, and even the darkness of the deep sleep—all are nothing but modifications of the mind. Consciousness, by whose light the individual is aware of these changes, remains unchanged. It illumines the known, and at the same time, remains unaffected by the content of the known. If Consciousness were to undergo any change, there would be no consistency in our experience from one state to another. Our own experience of the consistency of "I" is proof of the oneness of Consciousness that strings all the states together. The awareness of the differences between the three states further shows that the knower of the differences is unchanging.

Furthermore, Consciousness, the conscious knower of all states, does not need any faculty (senses or mind) to know or to illumine the content of each state. It is our everyday experience that in the waking state the senses are active, while in the dream state, the senses are inactive, but Consciousness still illumines our dreams, and in the deep sleep state, even the mind is inactive, yet still Consciousness continues to illumine (there, it illumines the absence of everything). Consciousness illumines itself also, for its very nature is to shine. It constantly vibrates in the heart (of experience) as "I am." Whoever becomes aware of his true nature as this pure Consciousness becomes fearless, referred to in this verse as the state of immortality (amṛta). The peace of such a person is thereby not affected by what transpires out in the world.

Meditation exercise

> As soon as you wake up from sleep, ask yourself "How do I know that a few moments ago I was asleep and now I am not?" Deeply contemplate the following: If I know that I was asleep and now I am awake, then that means "I" must be present during both sleep and waking. What is the nature of that "I"? Is it the body? But the physical body is not

> experienced in sleep. Or is it the mind? But the mind is not present in dreamless sleep. Absorb yourself in this inquiry of the "I" that illumines all states of consciousness.

This verse can also be interpreted in a slightly different way that can serve as a guiding light even in the most difficult situations of life. Each of us wants our life to take a certain course, but life flows in its own way, our preferences and judgments notwithstanding. We might like to change some situations that come our way, but the fact is that we often do not have the power to do so. This makes us feel helpless or powerless. However, instead of dwelling on the disappointment, frustration, or hurt, a seeker investigates the cause of the suffering. The answer that inevitably comes up is that an unpleasant situation has put a dent in one's imagined identity. That situation has challenged the individual's very identity. It has threatened his self-image and shaken him to the core. The expectation of a particular outcome—whether in a situation or in a relationship—is closely tied to the person's identity, and when that expectation is not met, it causes suffering. The situation may be external, but the emotion it brings up is internal. This does not justify unfairness, unkindness, or injustice in the external world, but it means that no matter how unfair, unkind, or unjust the world may be, the emotions that arise exist entirely within us. Our reactions and emotions reveal the extent of our understanding of ourselves.

Suffering can thus be used as a pointer to gauge how we see ourselves, and ultimately help us know our true nature, which can never be disturbed. In this way, every thought, every experience, every happening (pratibodha) is a teacher—provided we have the willingness to learn—that can help us get closer to our true identity. By seeing life situations not as a wall but as a doorway to understanding our true nature, we stop feeling powerless. Simply by changing our vision, instead of experiencing stress in worldly life (powerlessness), we gain strength or power (vīryam), and consequently, the deep-seated fear of life begins to dissolve (amṛta). True strength comes from this sādhanā, not from pumping iron, gaining a superior position, dominating others, or gaining recognition from others. A wise person who attains this strength lives each moment with a sense of joy, wonder and enthusiasm.

The outcome of the knowledge (*vidyā*) of one's true nature as Consciousness is fearlessness, described here as the nectar of immortality (amṛta). This does not give physical immortality, for that is impossible, but gives the realization that one's true Self is already immortal—eternal and boundless. It is rising above regarding oneself as a mere mortal human being.

self-effort → inner strength (vīryam)

Self-knowledge → fearlessness (amṛtam)

(Verse 2:4)

Meditation exercise

Think of an unpleasant situation you might be experiencing that you want to change but are unable to. Now, instead of dwelling on the frustration of not being able to fix it, think of how that situation might serve as a catalyst to facilitate your emotional growth. What lessons can you learn from it? What does it reveal about your understanding of yourself? How can you use that situation to come to know your true nature? In this way, offer gratitude for whatever is taking place in your life. Consider every moment and every situation as a divine blessing, and let that feeling of gratitude permeate your entire being.

Verse 5

इह चेदवेदीदथ सत्यमस्ति न चेदिहावेदीन्महती विनष्टिः ।
भूतेषु भूतेषु विचित्य धीराः प्रेत्यास्माल्लोकादमृता भवन्ति ॥ ५ ॥

(5) iha cedavedīdatha satyamasti na cedihāvedīnmahatī vinaṣṭiḥ,
bhūteṣu bhūteṣu vicitya dhīrāḥ pretyāsmāllokādamṛtā bhavanti.

Translation:
If a person comes to know (his true nature) here, then his life becomes authentic (fulfilled); if a person does not come to know (his true nature) in this life, then there is a great loss (for him). By seeing (that same Consciousness shining) in every being, the wise rise above this (dualistic experience of the) world and become immortal (fearless).

A PERSON who does not explore his true identity lives his life convinced of his identity as a helpless person, constantly struggling to find happiness in things, people, and situations. The strong notions of "me" and "mine" propel that person to be concerned only about his own pleasure. This small-mindedness, or unwillingness to share, is indeed the root of all personal, interpersonal, social, and global issues. Our true nature as Consciousness is boundless, so to live a life out of sync with that truth naturally leads to a life of inauthenticity. Over time, through this conditioning, a person's thoughts, speech, and actions become misaligned. Recognition of one's true identity as Consciousness brings about authenticity (*satya*, truth) in the individual. Such a being's thoughts, speech, and actions are in perfect alignment, as he lives a life of integrity, dignity, and generosity.

A person who is unaware of his true identity takes on false identities imposed on him by his surroundings. All of us have multiple roles to play, depending on our body (gender, age), relationships (father, mother, husband, wife, friend, and so on), occupation, and personality. All of these roles, albeit important, are temporary. They are not real, hence not satya (truth). They are simply roles we play, but to identify with them inevitably leads to suffering when we experience a little dent in any of them. Sooner or later, all our belongings, no matter how precious, will not be in our possession anymore, for either they will meet their end or we will meet ours. Sooner or later, all our loved ones will also part from us. Nothing that is considered mine in this moment will always be with me. To consider otherwise and to invest our identity and seek happiness and love in things and people is nothing but ignorance *(avidyā)*. Enjoyment of life is not being denied or condemned here, but clinging to life is being warned against. The body itself will die one day and disintegrate back into dust. With the departure of the life force from the body, the personality—no matter how flamboyant or impressive—disappears into thin air; all that is left is that personality in the memories of those who knew him, and with the passage of time, that too disappears.

Anything that is temporary cannot be considered real (satya), for it only appears real for the time being. The only principle that is truly real is Consciousness, the awareness of being, for that is ever present. No one can deny his being-ness at any time. Everything else comes and goes. To realize the eternal Consciousness as our true nature is the attainment of truth (satya). The highest potential of a human birth is this Self-realization, which can happen because the human incarnation has an intellect that allows us to explore our true nature. To live a pleasure-oriented life in a human body is truly a waste of the opportunity offered by a human birth. Even animals do that. To live a reflection-orientated life is in alignment with the potential of human birth, and to attain the knowledge of the Self (Self-knowledge-oriented life) is the fulfillment of human birth. This is termed *mokṣa*, freedom from suffering, from the cycle of birth and death (*saṁsāra*). It is only by divine grace and through lifetimes of spiritual practice that an individual experiences this beatitude of inner homecoming.

Possibilities of Human Birth

pleasure-oriented life	waste of human birth
reflection-oriented life	potential of human birth
Self-knowledge-oriented life	fulfillment of human birth

Meditation exercise

> Sit still and gently close your eyes. With a feeling of gratitude, reflect on your current embodiment as a human being and the possibilities that brings. Contemplate the remarkable faculties offered by a human body, especially the unique faculty of the intellect. What is the real purpose of your life? Do you want to live a humdrum life, frantically wandering in search of fleeting happiness, enjoying sense pleasures and suffering the pangs of unfulfilled desires, and then one day just drop dead? Or do you want to actualize your human potential to know the source of all life and experience eternal peace? Allow this questioning to bring mental clarity to the purpose of your existence.

The second half of the verse points to how this fulfillment has an impact on all those who come in contact with that wise being. The way one sees others is simply a reflection of the way one sees oneself. Whatever one sees within is what one sees without, for it is the same eye that sees in both cases. One who has recognized one's Self as Consciousness sees others as that, too; such a person sees them as not different from himself. He does not define others based on their weaknesses and faults, nor does he define anyone's identity based on appearance (body), personality (mind), or status (society). The more different the other is regarded from the self, the more difficult it becomes to relate to that person. Judgment is the root of all conflict. A wise being simply accepts the other's personality as it is, for he knows that the Consciousness enlivening him and the Consciousness enlivening the other are one and the same. The differences (*dvaita*) are superficial (*asatya*, unreal), whereas the non-difference (advaita) is real (satya). Such a knower becomes free from fear. He rises above the conflicts of everyday life (*pretyāsmāllokāt; pretya*, having risen; *asmāt*, from this; *lokāt*, world, experience).

In Advaita Vedānta, an analogy in the form of a story is often used to explain Self-knowledge. Once, in the darkness of night-time, a traveler sees a snake lying on the ground. He recoils and runs away in fear. As dawn breaks, he returns on the same path, and this time the light of the sun allows him to see clearly. He realizes he had made an error: what he perceived as a snake was in fact a garland.[9] With this knowledge, his fear vanishes. Similarly, in the light of Self-knowledge, the darkness of ignorance (or misunderstanding) and the consequent fear vanish. Then, the wise person no longer sees others as a snake to fight or run away from out of fear (fight-or-flight response), but instead sees them only as a garland to embrace out of divine love (amṛta). In reality, for a Self-realized being, everything is simply a different expression of that same Consciousness.

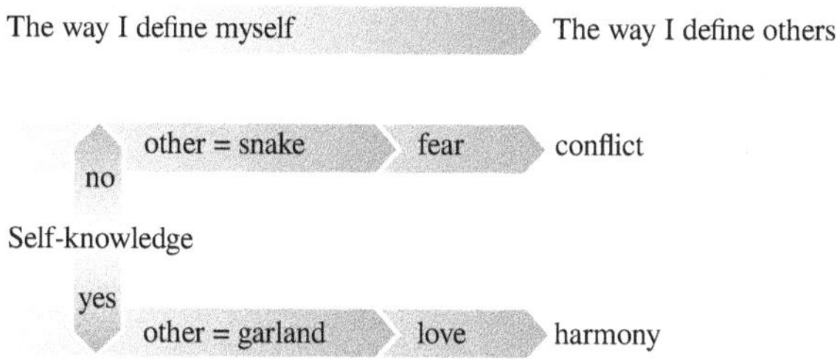

॥ इति द्वितीय खण्डः ॥

iti dvitīya khaṇḍaḥ.

Thus ends chapter two.

[9] According to a more popular version of the story, it is a rope.

CHAPTER THREE

The Story

"Can you blow this blade of grass?"

In this chapter, the teacher tells an entertaining story to symbolically explain the sublime principles shared thus far.

Verse 1

ब्रह्म ह देवेभ्यो विजिग्ये
तस्य ह ब्रह्मणो विजये देवा अमहीयन्त ॥ १ ॥

(1) brahma ha devebhyo vijigye
tasya ha brahmaṇo vijaye devā amahīyanta.

Translation:
(Teacher:) (Once upon a time,) Brahman verily obtained victory for the *devas* (gods or celestial forces) (in a battle over the *asuras*, demons or underground forces). The devas were overjoyed by the victory, which was really due to Brahman.

THE BATTLE between the devas and the asuras for wealth, women, and property is eternal, and stories of their conflict abound in the body of Hindu literature known as the *Purāṇas*. Whenever the devas win the battle, they get haughty, and their intoxication with hubris weakens them and makes them prone to another attack from the asuras. They come back to their senses, seek help from the divine, regain their lost wealth, but then succumb to arrogance once again. This cycle continues for eternity.

Verse 2

त ऐक्षन्तास्माकमेवायं विजयोऽस्माकमेवायं महिमेति ।
तद्धैषां विजज्ञौ तेभ्यो ह प्रादुर्बभूव
तन्न व्यजानत किमिदं यक्षमिति ॥ २ ॥

(2) ta aikṣantāsmākamevāyaṁ vijayo'smākamevāyaṁ mahimeti,
taddhaiṣāṁ vijajñau tebhyo ha prādurbabhūva
tanna vyajānata kimidaṁ yakṣamiti.

Translation:
They thought thus: “By us alone has this victory been obtained. This glory belongs only to us.” Knowing their (vanity), Brahman

appeared before them. The (devas) could not understand who that spirit (*yakśa*) was.

THE MYSTERIOUS spirit was so enchanting that it drew the attention of the intoxicated devas away from their celebration and aroused their curiosity to inquire into the spirit's identity.

Verse 3

तेऽग्निमब्रुवञ्जातवेद एतद्विजानीहि
किमिदं यक्षमिति तथेति ॥ ३ ॥

(3) te'gnimabruvañjātaveda etadvijānīhi
kimidaṁ yakṣamiti tatheti.

Translation:
They said to Agni (the fire god), "O omniscient one, find out who this spirit is." "Yes," (said Agni).

FIRE is associated with the sense organs, and since it is through the senses that we gain knowledge of the world around us, Agni is given the epithet "the omniscient one" (*jātaveda*).

Verse 4

तदभ्यद्रवत्तमभ्यवदत्कोऽसीति अग्निर्वा
अहमस्मीत्यब्रवीज्जातवेदा वा अहमस्मीति ॥ ४ ॥

(4) tadabhyadravattamabhyavadatko'sīti agnirvā
ahamasmītyabravījjātavedā vā ahamasmīti.

Translation:
Agni rushed to that spirit. (The spirit asked,) "Who are you?" (Agni replied haughtily,) "I am Agni, the omniscient one."

SUCH WAS the power of the spirit's presence that before Agni could question the spirit's identity, the spirit questioned Agni's. Agni's haughty answer reveals his arrogance. Instead of simply giving his name, Agni gave his title, suggesting that everyone should know who he was because of his high stature. This is one of the prime symptoms of lack of Self-knowledge.

Verse 5

तस्मिंस्त्वयि किं वीर्यमित्यपीदꣳ सर्वं
दहेयं यदिदं पृथिव्यामिति ॥ ५ ॥

(5) tasmiṁstvayi kiṁ vīryamityapīdaṁ sarvaṁ
daheyaṁ yadidaṁ pṛthivyāmiti.

Translation:
(The spirit asked,) "What power do you who is of such glory have?" "I can burn up all that exists on earth," (Agni replied).

CLEARLY, the spirit was testing the extent of Agni's vanity. Agni claimed he had such power that he could make anything into nothing. Because he could turn anything into ashes, Agni considered himself omnipotent.

Verse 6

तस्मै तृणं निदधावेतद्दहेति ।
तदुपप्रेयाय सर्वजवेन तन्न शशाक दग्धुं
स तत एव निववृते
नैतदशकं विज्ञातुं यदेतद्यक्षमिति ॥ ६ ॥

(6) tasmai tṛṇaṁ nidadhāvetaddaheti,
tadupapreyāya sarvajavena tanna śaśāka dagdhuṁ
sa tata eva nivavṛte
naitadaśakaṁ vijñātuṁ yadetadyakṣamiti.

Translation:
(The spirit) placed a blade of grass before him and said, "Burn this." (Agni) rushed toward it with all his might, but could not burn it (even a bit). He returned (to the devas) and said, "I could not find who that spirit was."

AGNI RETURNED to the devas embarrassed and surprised. His claim of omniscience and omnipotence was not only challenged but rendered bogus. Without sharing any details about the encounter, he simply reported his ignorance of the spirit's identity.

Verse 7

अथ वायुमब्रुवन्वायवेतद्विजानीहि
किमेतद्यक्षमिति तथेति ॥ ७ ॥

(7) atha vāyumabruvanvāyavetadvijānīhi
kimetadyakṣamiti tatheti.

Translation:
(The gods) then said to Vāyu (the wind god), "O god of wind, find out who this spirit is." "Yes," (said Vāyu).

THE GODS sent the heavenly being who was next in their hierarchy, namely Vāyu, the wind god.

Verse 8

तदभ्यद्रवत्तमभ्यवदत्कोऽसीति वायुर्वा
अहमस्मीत्यब्रवीन्मातरिश्वा वा अहमस्मीति ॥ ८ ॥

(8) tadabhyadravattamabhyavadatko'sīti vāyurvā
ahamasmītyabravīnmātariśvā vā ahamasmīti.

Translation:
(Vāyu also) rushed to that spirit. (The spirit asked,) "Who are you?" (Vāyu replied haughtily,) "I am Vāyu, the one who treads the skies."

VĀYU'S WORDS contain the same arrogance that was sensed in Agni's words. Wind is associated with the mind, and since the mind can travel anywhere instantly, Vāyu is given the epithet the "one who treads the skies" (*mātariśva*).

While Agni's epithet (jātaveda, the omniscient one) revealed that he considered himself omniscient, Vāyu's epithet (mātariśva, the one who treads the skies) reveals that he considered himself omnipresent.

Verse 9

तस्मिंस्त्वयि किं वीर्यमित्यपीदं
सर्वमाददीय यदिदं पृथिव्यामिति ॥ ९ ॥

(9) tasmiṁstvayi kiṁ vīryamityapīdaṁ
sarvamādadīya yadidaṁ pṛthivyāmiti.

Translation:
(The spirit asked,) "What power do you who is of such glory have?" "I can blow away everything that exists on earth," (Vāyu replied).

THE SPIRIT tested Vāyu's vanity, just as he did with Agni. From Vāyu's arrogant reply, it is clear he considered himself powerful because he could displace anything from anywhere. He believed that everything was held in place only because of him. Like Agni, he also considered himself omnipotent.

Verse 10

तस्मै तृणं निदधावेतदादत्स्वेति
तदुपप्रेयाय सर्वजवेन तन्न शशाकादातुं
स तत एव निववृते
नैतदशकं विज्ञातुं यदेतद्यक्षमिति ॥ १० ॥

(10) tasmai tṛṇaṁ nidadhāvetadādatsveti
tadupapreyāya sarvajavena tanna śaśākādātuṁ
sa tata eva nivavṛte
naitadaśakaṁ vijñātuṁ yadetadyakṣamiti.

Translation:
The spirit placed a blade of grass before him and said, "Blow this away." (Vāyu) rushed toward it with all his might, but could not move it (even an inch). Thence he returned (to the devas) and said, "I could not find out who that spirit was."

THE SEQUENCE of events that transpired with Agni was repeated with Vāyu. Ignorance was perpetuated, as Agni was too proud to share the details about his embarrassing defeat and Vāyu was too proud to ask and learn from Agni's experience. Humility to share one's life experiences and humility to learn from others' life experiences are the key to gaining a deep understanding of life.

Verse 11

अथेन्द्रमब्रुवन्मघवन्नेतद्विजानीहि
किमेतद्यक्षमिति तथेति तदभ्यद्रवत्तस्मात्तिरोदधे ॥ ११ ॥

(11) athendramabruvanmaghavannetadvijānīhi
kimetadyakṣamiti tatheti tadabhyadravattasmāttirodadhe.

Translation:
Then (the gods) said to Indra (the king of the gods), "O possessor of great wealth, find out who this spirit is." "Yes," (said Indra). He (also) rushed to that spirit, but the spirit disappeared thence.

INDRA SITS on the heavenly throne as the king of the gods. He is addressed as the "possessor of great wealth" (*maghavan*) because the heaven where the gods reside (*svarga*) is the land of pleasure, and being the king of that region, he is the owner of all the material riches that reside there, including the wish-fulfilling tree. There is no material desire that cannot be fulfilled in heaven.

Indra was summoned as the last resort to investigate into the spirit's identity. As soon as Indra reached the scene, the spirit playfully disappeared.

Verse 12

स तस्मिन्नेवाकाशे स्त्रियमाजगाम
बहुशोभमानामुमाँ हैमवतीं
ताँहोवाच किमेतद्यक्षमिति ॥ १२ ॥

(12) sa tasminnevākāśe striyamājagāma
bahuśobhamānāmumāṁ haimavatīṁ
tāṁhovāca kimetadyakṣamiti.

Translation:
In that same place (where the spirit had been), Indra saw an extremely beautiful woman, Umā Haimavatī (goddess). To her he asked, "Who is this spirit?"

HAIMAVATĪ, the "daughter of Himavān (the personification of the Himalayas)," is one of the names of the goddess Umā who is the consort of Śiva (God).

Indra's demeanor reflects humility, unlike that of Agni and Vāyu, who preceded him in the inquiry. This will open up the door to wisdom for him.

। इति तृतीय खण्डः ॥

iti tṛtīya khaṇḍaḥ.

Thus ends chapter three.

CHAPTER FOUR

The Practice

“What is the *Upaniṣad*, really?”

In this chapter, the teacher gives some powerful practices to enable the students to embody the spirit of the *Upaniṣad* while living in the world.

Verse 1

सा ब्रह्मेति होवाच
ब्रह्मणो वा एतद्विजये महीयध्वमिति
ततो हैव विदाञ्चकार ब्रह्मेति ॥ १ ॥

(1) sā brahmeti hovāca
brahmaṇo vā etadvijaye mahīyadhvamiti
tato haiva vidāñcakāra brahmeti.

Translation:
(Teacher:) She said, "It is Brahman! It is indeed through Brahman's victory that you have gained glory." Then alone (Indra) understood (that the spirit was) Brahman.[10]

THE PURPOSE of this story is to symbolically explain the ideas communicated directly hitherto. The mantras (*Upaniṣad* verses) thus far conveyed the philosophy in a direct way, while this story conveys the same in an indirect and entertaining way. Mantras or *sūtras* (aphorisms) and *kathās* (sacred stories) are the two main modes of communication in the Vedic tradition. This story, like any in the Vedic scriptures, is open to interpretation; everyone interprets it in his own way, in a way that makes sense to him.

Agni (the fire god) represents the eyes because the element (*mahābhūta*) fire is associated with the subtle element (*tanmātra*) of form (rūpa). Agni is also considered the deity of speech. The eyes stand for the organs of perception (*jñānendriya*), and speech for the organs of action (*karmendriya*). Collectively, Agni represents the sense organs (eyes, ears, tongue, nose, and skin) that interact with the outer world, which is nothing but a collection of names (nāma, words spoken by the tongue) and forms (rūpa, objects seen by the eyes).

Vāyu (the wind god) represents not only the breath but also the mind, for the speed of the mind reminds us of the element wind.

[10] In his lectures on the *Kena Upaniṣad*, Swami Chinmayananda mentions that Brahman taking the form of a yakśa illustrates the concept of avatar (divine incarnation), which was elaborated later in the *Purāṇas*.

The connection between the breath and the mind is not just well documented but also everyone's personal experience: when the mind is agitated, breathing is rapid and shallow, and when the mind is relaxed, breathing is slow and deep.

Whereas Agni represents the physical body, Vāyu represents the subtle body. Together, they cover all the faculties of the human body. Indra is the king of the devas, so he represents the ego-sense (ahaṁkāra), the deep, visceral feeling "I am this limited person," which dictates the use of the mind and senses to seek pleasure in the field of sense objects.

The victory of the devas over the asuras symbolizes the cultivation of virtues and the victory over vices (animal instincts) in a person. In the initial stages of sādhanā, the danger of feeling nobler than others (spiritual pride) is almost inevitable. This is shown in the story by the devas thinking they obtained victory because of their own merit and power. This is delusion. Although a seeker's self-effort is a must on the spiritual path, any progress is only due to divine grace—the invisible hand guiding, protecting, and propelling the seeker forward. This is pointed out in the story by stating that the devas obtained victory only due to Brahman.

When virtues predominate in an individual, and he is ready to walk the path of self-inquiry, the divine comes into his life in some way (usually in the form of a Guru) and gives him an initial vision (*darśana*) of the divine, supreme principle (Brahman, pure Consciousness), represented here as the mysterious spirit (yakśa). This powerful experience sets the person off on self-inquiry, as narrated in this story.

That pure Consciousness is beyond the reach of the senses (Agni) and the mind (Vāyu), and beyond the physical body (Agni) and the subtle body (Vāyu). It is only because of Consciousness that the senses and the mind can function, so how can they behold Consciousness? This is the reason Agni and Vāyu could not burn or move even a blade of grass.

The senses and the mind can only behold names and forms, not their source, which is beyond them. Knowledge obtained via the senses and the mind is indirect knowledge. Consciousness cannot be known indirectly because Consciousness is not an object of experience, but rather the experiencer itself. It can only be known directly as one's own being, the pure Awareness "I am." Just as when Indra inquired into the spirit, the spirit disappeared, so when the ego directly inquires into its source, it realizes the truth that Consciousness is not an object to be perceived outside. The individual has to dive deep within. When the individual makes an effort through self-inquiry, God's grace (*śakti*, divine power, inner power), represented in the story by Umā (goddess), guides the seeker toward the truth of his own nature. The illumination comes from the śakti seated within. In deep meditation, the illumination dawns that Brahman, Consciousness, is the source and substance of all there is. While the ignorant fruitlessly chase after things and people for happiness, the wise seek the nature of Consciousness, the source of both spiritual attainment and material success.

Character (Chapter 3)	**Represents**
Agni (fire)	eyes (organs of perception) speech (organs of action) ∴ physical body
Vāyu (air)	breath mind ∴ subtle body
Indra (king of devas)	ego
devas (gods or celestial forces)	virtues
asuras (demons or underground forces)	vices
yakśa (mysterious spirit)	pure Consciousness (Brahman)
Umā (goddess)	grace

The plot also lends itself to a comparison with the sequence of creation, for the story is about inquiry into the source of the self, which is the same as the source of all creation. The order in which the characters appear during the inquiry phase is the reverse of the order for creation, namely: fire (Agni), air (Vāyu), space (Indra), śakti (the power of Brahman, Umā) that creates duality as delusion (māyā) but also dissolves duality as grace (*anugraha*), and finally Brahman (pure Consciousness, yakśa). During self-inquiry, the individual goes through this sequence, starting with awareness of the world (earth and water); then of his body (fire); then of his mind (air); then of his ego (space); and then of his inner power (śakti), which points to his true Self (Brahman).

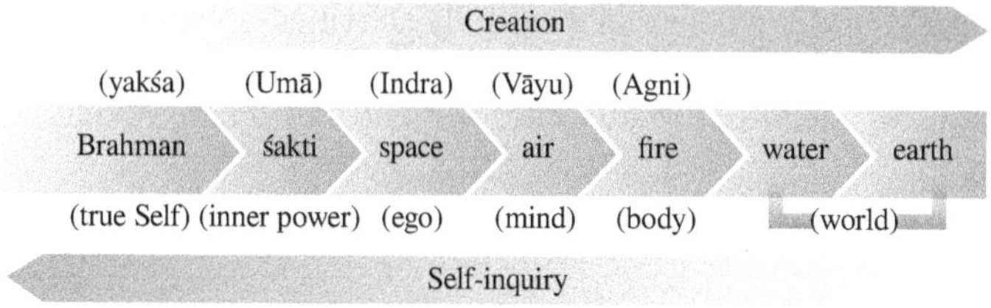

Finally, the story can also be simplified to mean that we are all instruments in the game of the divine. Not even a blade of grass can move without the will of the divine. A firm conviction about this knowledge brings about true humility in conjunction with a loving acceptance of everything as it is.

Verse 2

तस्माद्वा एते देवो अतितरामिवान्यान्देवान्यदग्निर्वायुरिन्द्रस्ते
ह्येनन्नेदिष्ठं पस्पृशुस्ते ह्येनत्प्रथमो विदाञ्चकार ब्रह्मेति ॥ २ ॥

(2) tasmādvā ete devo atitarāmivānyāndevānyadag-nirvāyurindraste
hyenannediṣṭhaṁ paspṛśuste hyenatprathamo vidāñcakāra brahmeti.

Translation:
Therefore, these gods—Agni, Vāyu, and Indra—are indeed superior to the other gods, for they approached nearest (to the spirit, Brahman in disguise) and were the first to know it as Brahman.

THIS VERSE extols the glory of those who pursue self-inquiry. Very few in the human population are interested in inquiring into the nature of the Self. Most are so enamored by things, people, and events—their resultant suffering notwithstanding—that they hardly even think of turning the mind within. Here, the teacher metaphorically shares that the mere effort to investigate the Self yields tremendous benefit. Those who turn within truly excel in life, for they become not just more content but also more efficient in their daily activities. Decrease in stress and increase in efficiency are some of the side benefits of self-inquiry. Excellence in the outer world is then a natural outcome.

Verse 3

तस्माद्वा इन्द्रोऽतितरामिवान्यान्देवान्स
ह्येनन्नेदिष्ठं पस्पर्श
स ह्येनत्प्रथमो विदाञ्चकार ब्रह्मेति ॥ ३ ॥

(3) tasmādvā indro'titarāmivānyāndevānsa
hyenannediṣṭhaṁ pasparśa
sa hyenatprathamo vidāñcakāra brahmeti.

Translation:
Therefore, Indra surpasses the other gods, for he approached nearest (to the spirit) and was the first to know it as Brahman.

THIS VERSE extols the glory of those who realize the nature of the Self. Great are those who pursue self-inquiry, and greater even are those who realize the true nature of the Self as Brahman, pure Consciousness. There is nothing higher than Self-knowledge, so the one who attains it is nothing but divinity personified. The identity of such a being is no longer limited to the individual personality.

Meditation exercise

Sit and gently close your eyes. Tell (and retell) this story to your own mind. As you narrate and imagine the story, contemplate the significance of each character and event. What does each character and event signify to you? What lessons can you draw from the story? How is the story relevant to your life and sādhanā?

Verse 4

तस्यैष आदेशो
यदेतद्विद्युतो व्यद्युतदा ३ इतीन्न्यमीमिषदा ३
इत्यधिदैवतम् ॥ ४ ॥

(4) tasyaiṣa ādeśo
yadetadvidyuto vyadyutadā 3[11] *itīnnyamīmiṣadā 3*
ityadhidaivatam.

Translation:
This illustration of that (Brahman) is given: That is like a flash of lightning. That is like the blinking of an eye. This is with reference to nature as divine.

THE COMPASSIONATE teacher tries another approach here. He gives two examples that can be observed by the seeker in his everyday life: one in the natural world (lightning) and the other in the body (blinking). Understanding a story requires some analysis, which realistically might not be everyone's cup of tea. But everyone can have a direct experience of these two examples, so the teacher uses them to explain Brahman and to

[11] The symbol "3" indicates an overlong vowel in Sanskrit (*pluta*) and is perhaps used by the teacher here to emphasize the two observations he shares. It reveals the teacher's zeal to impart Self-knowledge to the student.

help the student become firmly anchored in the experience of the truth he has experienced within his own heart. The first example given is a flash of lightning. Anyone who has seen lightning strike knows it is a spontaneous happening; its exact moment of occurrence is unpredictable. It comes all of a sudden and lasts only for an instant. The second example given is the blinking of an eye. While lightning is rare and momentary, blinking is ordinary and continual—the exact opposite.

Like lightning, Consciousness is farther than the farthest, for it is beyond the reach of the senses and the mind; however, like blinking, it is closer than the closest, for it is within one's own being. While the recognition of Consciousness comes through the grace of the divine (from above, like lightning), it also requires tremendous effort on the part of the seeker (from below, like blinking). The first direct glimpse of one's true nature as Consciousness comes like a flash of lightning: it is sudden, momentary, a special moment. But true attainment lies in making this experience like the blinking of an eye: a continual aspect, one's natural state. The recognition of one's true Self dawns in an instant (like lightning), but at the same time, that recognition is of the fact that the supreme principle has always been present (like blinking) as the Self; it is nothing new, nothing foreign, nothing distant, for it is one's own being, "I am." This is a divine paradox!

Brahman (pure Consciousness)

Flash of lightning	Blinking of an eye
• farther than the farthest	• closer than the closest
• grace of the divine	• effort of the seeker
• a special moment	• a natural state
• instant recognition	• always present

(Verse 4:4)

Observation of the world around us is not just a powerful but also an essential practice for inner growth. In the lineage of the Gurus, the first Guru, Dattātreya, gained wisdom simply by observing nature. This means nature can be the ultimate teacher if we have the eyes to see what it shows and the ears to hear what it says. The entire body of the *Vedas* is considered to be "that which is heard" (śruti), which means the ancient sages heard the eternal wisdom resonating in nature. It was not created by anyone's mind. To listen to nature and the world around us, we have to be silent, both in speech and in mind. The deeper the inner silence, the more we can learn.

Meditation exercise

> Go for a walk in nature by yourself. Do not take any gadgets or books with you, either. As you saunter, observe the sights of nature with open eyes and listen to the sounds of nature with open ears. Observe and listen with a clear mind, without trying to label or explain anything. Behold the diversity of nature—so intricate in design and yet so simple in its principle. What lessons can you learn from the natural world? As you reflect on this question, begin to feel that you, too, are a part and parcel of that same nature. So, what separates your connection to nature?

Verse 5

अथाध्यात्मं यदेतद्गच्छतीव च मनोऽनेन
चैतदुपस्मरत्यभीक्ष्णꣳ सङ्कल्पः ॥ ५ ॥

(5) athādhyātmaṁ yadetadgacchatīva ca mano'nena
caitadupasmaratyabhīkṣṇaṁ saṅkalpaḥ.

Translation:
Now, this (illustration) from the inner world is given: (observe) the speed with which the mind thinks (and continually) goes from one thought to another.

IN THE PREVIOUS verse, the teacher showed the student how acute observation of one's natural world can point to the supreme principle; in this one, he is showing the student how acute observation of one's own mind can give the experience of the supreme principle. The teaching of observation is common to both, but what is being observed is different: in the previous verse, it was the outer world; in this one, it is the inner world.

The practice suggested here is a direct observation of the movements of the mind. Right off the bat, this demands a shift in our attention from outside to inside, the first step to meditation. The first observation any meditator makes is the speed with which the mind moves, to the extent that it seems impossible to ever get it under control. The teacher comments on the speed of the mind but does not leave it at that, for that would dishearten the student. He gives a hint to find the stillness within; namely, that the mind goes from one thought to another. This means that between the end of one thought and the beginning of the next thought, there is a pause, imperceptible but very much present. In this gap, there is no thought, hence no world (to cause any sorrow) either. This gap is the supreme principle, Brahman. While the first observation regarding the speed of the mind points to the realization of the supreme principle as a herculean task, the second observation about the gap between thoughts points to it being an effortless task. The supreme principle is right here, right now—so close that even thinking is not required; in fact, thinking is itself the biggest hindrance.

In total, four observations are given as centering techniques: two from outside (verse 4.4) and two from inside (4.5), and they progressively transition from the outermost to the innermost: flash of lightning (nature); blinking of an eye (body); thoughts (mind); and finally, the space between thoughts (Consciousness).

Meditation exercise

> Find a space of quiet. Adopt a comfortable posture, with the only requirement being a straight spine, and your neck in alignment with it. Turn your attention away from objects outside and toward

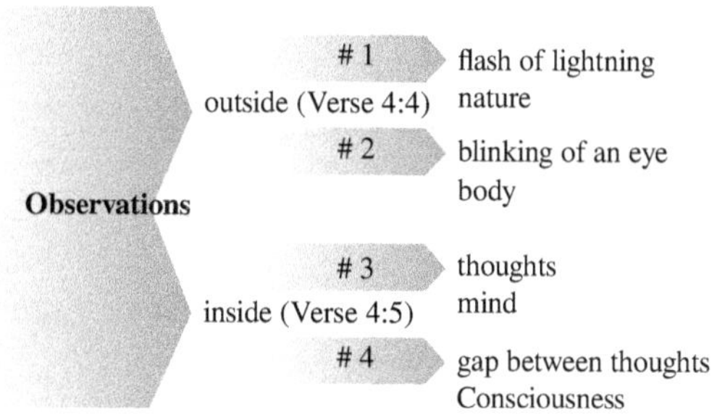

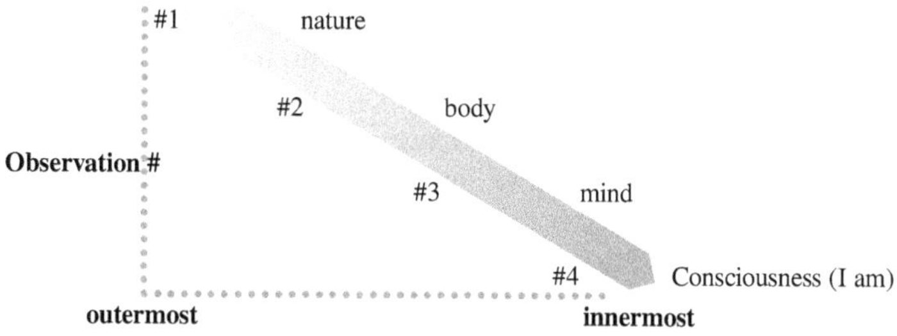

thoughts inside. Without judging the quality of any thought, just notice its existence. Become aware of the incredible speed at which the mind thinks, due to the thoughts occurring in succession. No sooner than one thought ends, another begins. However, there has to be a pause between the two, even if it is very brief. After one thought ends and before the next begins, there is a gap. Turn your attention away from the thoughts and toward this mysterious and elusive gap. What exists in that gap between any two thoughts? Absorb yourself in this investigation.

Verse 6

तद्ध तद्वनं नाम तद्वनमित्युपासितव्यं
स य एतदेवं वेदाभि हैनं
सर्वाणि भूतानि संवाञ्छन्ति ॥ ६ ॥

(6) taddha tadvanaṁ nāma tadvanamityupāsitavyaṁ
sa ya etadevaṁ vedābhi hainaṁ
sarvāṇi bhūtāni saṁvāñchanti.

Translation:
That (Brahman) is known by the name *tadvana* (the one who is loved by all); thus, it is to be worshipped as *tadvana* (the one who is loved by all). All beings long for one (who has this knowledge).

THE SOURCE of life is love. Love is, in fact, only for the Self. One loves oneself the most, and it is this love for oneself that drives a person to seek happiness, no matter where.[12] After a day of engagement in the world outside, we feel exhausted and crave a restful sleep. No matter how much we love any person or thing, to experience the joy of deep sleep, we let go of it all. This shows that ultimately we love our own Self the most; hence, Brahman (Self) is known by the name *tadvana*, the "one who is loved by all."

Everyone seeks happiness at all times because that is the nature of the Self; namely, joy (*ānanda*). Happiness does not lie in anything outside. Something that gives rise to happiness in one person can give rise to indifference in another, and even sadness in another. In fact, the same person can give someone happiness at one time and grief at another time. No sense experience has ever given anyone the same measure of happiness at all times. That is a clue that happiness does not reside in objects. The happiness experienced in sense pleasures is only a reflection of the inherent happiness of the Self. Even though there are no attainable objects in deep sleep, we feel a joy that rejuvenates us

[12] This is explained in the *Bṛhadāraṇyaka Upaniṣad,* chapter 2, fourth Brāhmaṇa.

as nothing else can. A wise person realizes this, and instead of seeking happiness outside, seeks it within as his own true nature. Such a being becomes content within the Self. Not only that, he radiates that contentment outside. Whatever one has inside is what one radiates outside. A miserable person carries misery, and a happy person carries happiness.

Meditation exercise

> Notice that every life form, through various activities, is seeking only happiness. The source of that happiness is the Self. With a firm conviction of this understanding, turn the mind away from all its preoccupations and cravings and become absorbed in the innate joy of the Self.

Because we are drawn to that which provides us with the feeling of happiness, we feel a mysterious attraction to a person who has realized his true nature and revels in that inner peace. What we are attracted to is not the person but the peace radiating from that person. Self-realized beings—regardless of their gender, personality, occupation, or status—have an undeniable magnetism about them. Even their words and look have an awesome, charismatic, and endearing quality. Everything they say and do radiates a sense of holiness because it is infused with the power of their Self-knowledge. This mysterious phenomenon is difficult to convey in words, but anyone who has had the great fortune of being in the presence of an enlightened being—not necessarily in his physical company, but even through his words or photographs—knows the truth of this by personal experience.

For this reason, meditation on the Guru is one of the most effective techniques to calm the mind. The qualities of that upon which we meditate enter us; by meditating on the Guru, his exalted state begins to enter us. A Guru's entire being emanates such great power that even after departure from this world, his burial place (*samādhi* shrine) emanates the power (śakti) of meditation, and people flock there to receive blessings and guidance. A knower of the Self loves all, and all love him.[13]

Meditation exercise

> Gently close your eyes and mentally invoke your Guru, the teacher who awakened you to the vast treasure within you.[14] Bring to your mind his form: his smile, his laughter, his eyes, his gait, his touch, and all his characteristics. Remember his words: the mantra he gave, his teachings, his sayings, his voice, and his singing. Fill your mind with his form and his words. Fill every pore of your body with the remembrance of his universal compassion and unconditional love. Now imagine the state he lives in—immersed in the joy of his own Self, free from the pull of the mind and the senses, and enjoying every moment of life as a divine play. Absorb yourself in this state. Lose yourself and let the state of the Guru permeate your entire being.[15]

While ordinary individuals run after people, wealth, success, and other things of this world, the wise only run after knowledge of the Self, and when they do so, worldly benefits naturally follow, if that is destined to happen. Spiritual attainment and material success are not mutually exclusive, as assumed by many. However, sincerity in the quest for the former is essential to truly appreciate the benefits of either.

[13] This does not mean no one will be against a Self-realized being; indeed, such beings often become the object of jealousy and even hatred. However, that is due to the mental conditioning of those who feel that negativity; if they look beyond their prejudices, they, too, will recognize a divine pull toward the Self-realized being.

[14] If you have not yet found your Guru, this meditation exercise can be done on a deity (male or female) or even an ideal you may have.

[15] To know more about this mysterious meditation, see *Play of Consciousness*, Baba Muktananda's spiritual autobiography.

Verse 7

उपनिषदं भो ब्रूहीत्युक्ता त उपनिषद्ब्राह्मीं
वाव त उपनिषदमब्रूमेति ॥ ७ ॥

(7) upaniṣadaṁ bho brūhītyuktā ta upaniṣadbrāhmīṁ
vāva ta upaniṣadamabrūmeti.

Translation:
(Student:) O teacher, teach me the *Upaniṣad* (ultimate knowledge). (Teacher:) The *Upaniṣad* has been taught to you. We have certainly taught you the *Upaniṣad* about Brahman.

AT THIS POINT in the conversation, the student asks a question that can baffle anyone. He asks, "O teacher, can you teach me the *Upaniṣad*?" This makes one wonder if this student did not understand anything the teacher has communicated thus far. Or is there perhaps a deeper meaning to his question? In this verse, the teacher, as expected, answers that he has shared everything he knows, everything that is worth knowing. Truly speaking, besides knowledge of the Self, there is nothing else worth knowing.

There is a mysterious but an undeniable connection between a true teacher and a devoted disciple. Such a teacher can hear not only the student's spoken words but also his unspoken words and the meaning behind them. The teacher's answer in the following verse reveals his knowledge of the deeper meaning of the student's question.

Verse 8

तस्यै तपो दमः कर्मेति प्रतिष्ठा
वेदाः सर्वाङ्गानि सत्यमायतनम् ॥ ८ ॥

(8) tasyai tapo damaḥ karmeti pratiṣṭhā
vedāḥ sarvāṅgāni satyamāyatanam.

Translation:
Endurance, self-control, and selfless action are the foundations (of the *Upaniṣad*). All (four) *Vedas* are its pillars. Truth (the true Self) is its abode.

THIS ANSWER by the teacher shows that he understood the real intent behind the student's question. The student wants to hear from the teacher's mouth the practical application of the *Upaniṣad* in daily life. Furthermore, thus far, the teacher has imparted to the student a direct glimpse of the Self in multiple ways; the student now desires to make that experience permanent. Some seekers get lost in discussing sublime philosophy and forget to apply it in practice, and some get a glimpse but then do not follow up to integrate that experience in daily life. This student does not belong to either of these categories. He knows that the *Upaniṣad* is not for theoretical study and that its sole purpose is to give the experience of Self-knowledge—not just for a moment but permanently. For that, the seeker has to program his lifestyle a certain way. To succeed in any endeavor, one has to mold one's life in a particular way. Take the example of an athlete of any sport. He has to design his entire life, from diet to sleep to practice, so it is conducive to his eventual excellence. In the same way, a seeker's entire lifestyle has to be conducive for his spiritual practice (sādhanā).

The teacher imparts this final teaching by invoking the image of sādhanā (or the *Upaniṣad*) as a temple. The three foundations of this temple are penance or endurance (*tapa*), self-control (*dama*), and (selfless) action (*karma*). *Tapa* means the ability to tolerate difficulties without complaining. External conditions are not always pleasant, whether it is weather, neighbors, or any situation. Rather than complain or blame, he who aims to unfold his highest potential has to learn to endure it, knowing that "this too shall pass." Not everything is to our liking or in line with our preferences. *Tapa* thus means we need to learn to resist the feeling of aversion.

Next, the seeker is advised to curb his craving for pleasure. This ability to exercise self-control is called *dama*. The adage "no pain, no gain" applies across all fields. Struggle is necessary to bring out the best from within anyone, in any endeavor. This is not different in sādhanā. Self-discipline applies in all areas of life, and two important areas are diet and speech, both functions of the tongue. Usually we eat for taste and speak to feel important. Self-discipline in diet means we need to eat with a spirit of offering to the divine and not only for the satisfaction of our palate. This includes observing a vegetarian diet (most conducive for meditation) cooked from healthy and fresh ingredients, in clean vessels, and with affection. Speech must be "honest, beneficial, and pleasing" (*Bhagavad Gītā*, 17.15). A check of these guidelines before words are uttered might eliminate most of our conversations. If it's not necessary to speak, a seeker must refrain from it. The practice of silence is highly recommended because it conserves energy and helps one observe one's own thought patterns. With regard to sleep, moderation is recommended. Following a punctual schedule for meals and sleep helps keep the immune system boosted and the mind balanced. A seeker's surroundings must be kept clean and uncluttered. The body must also be kept clean. Many other guidelines for how to live a wholesome lifestyle are provided in scriptures such as the *Bhagavad Gītā* and *Yoga Sūtras (The Aphorisms on Yoga)*. These are not commandments, and there is no punishment for not abiding by them; they are simply guidelines set forth for those wishing to unfold their highest potential. Just as a tennis player follows a certain regime to excel in his sport, so we as seekers are advised to follow a certain regime to attain the knowledge of our true Self.

The third and last foundation is *karma*, or selfless action. When the seeker begins to reduce his aversion (*dveśa*) by tapa and attraction (*rāga*) by dama, then naturally his actions will be less motivated by selfishness. The intention behind the act then becomes not "for my pleasure," but "for the welfare of others." This is elaborated in the *Bhagavad Gītā*, where Śrī Kṛṣṇa explains that yoga involves performing an action wholeheartedly, and then fully accepting the outcome, whatever it may be, pleasant or unpleasant. This is the key to keeping equanimity in the face of life's highs and lows. When there is no expectation, how can there be any room for sorrow? For such a person, every act becomes an act of worship.

The pillars, or limbs, of spiritual practice are the *Vedas*. *Veda* refers to both the sacred textual source of the Vedic philosophy and to knowledge in general. There are four *Vedas* (*Ṛg, Yajur, Sāma*, and *Atharva*); thus, the temple of sādhanā has four pillars. Study of the sacred texts is known in Sanskrit as *svādhyāya*, which literally means self-study. The three foundations give us tips for how to act in the world with a balanced mind. But we also need a private practice, where we sit by ourselves and study our own mind and self. That daily personal practice in solitude is the pillar. The sages have devised a variety of personal practices: meditation (*dhyāna*), group chanting of the name of God (*kīrtana*), scriptural study (svādhyāya), mantra repetition (*japa*), hatha yoga, and many others. A seeker has the freedom to choose whatever suits his temperament, whatever works for him. The most important thing is that we have at least one practice, and that we stick with it until it yields its fullest benefit. Promiscuity in practice does not give the complete benefit of any. This daily practice forms our anchor. If we conduct ourselves in the world as pointed out in the three foundations, then our meditation (the pillar) gets stronger and stronger day by day, and as our meditation gets stronger, we become more balanced in daily life.

Finally, the abode or the altar in the sanctum sanctorum is truth (satya), the true Self. The *Upaniṣad* has already used this word in the context of the attainment of sādhanā.[16] The teacher uses it again here to reiterate the point. By penance, self-control, selfless work, and a daily practice of meditation, the seeker becomes more and more authentic (satya) and selfless in his thought, speech, and action. The stronger the connection with one's unchanging Self (satya), or pure Consciousness, the more one's thoughts, words, and acts will emerge from a space of large-heartedness.

[16] Verse 2.5

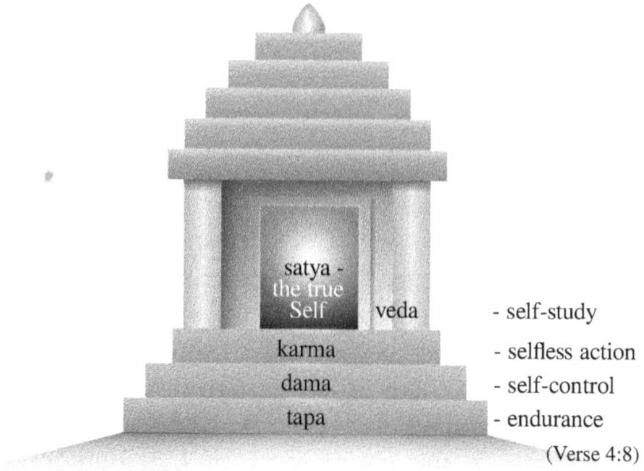

Verse 9

**यो वा एतामेवं वेदापहत्य पाप्मानमनन्ते
स्वर्गे लोके ज्येये प्रतितिष्ठति प्रतितिष्ठति ॥ ९ ॥**

*(9) yo vā etāmevaṁ vedāpahatya pāpmānamanante
svarge loke jyeye pratitiṣṭhati pratitiṣṭhati.*

Translation:
Verily, he who knows this (*Upaniṣad*) destroys all limitations (and) is thus established in the highest (principle), eternal heaven (the state of boundless joy). He is certainly established there!

THE *KENA UPANIṢAD* ends with an emphatic declaration that there is nothing higher than knowledge of the Self. Often inaccurately translated as "sin," the word *pāpa* does not have an English equivalent. *Pāpa* means the impressions of past actions and thoughts that keep the individual limited. It is the conditioning that keeps a person bound by his notions of "me," "mine," and "not mine." Knowledge of the Self destroys these fetters and the consequent suffering. The result is naturally an ever-present joy that has no limit and no end (eternal heaven). To emphasize that this indeed is the state of a Self-realized being, the teacher repeats the last word twice: *pratitiṣṭhati, pratitiṣṭhati* (established, established).

When we honestly analyze our own experience of life, we realize that everything comes and goes. Consciousness alone abides as the eternal presence. Clinging to anything that is impermanent is a recipe for misery. On the other hand, discovery of one's true Self as pure Consciousness brings about peace within—an eternal peace that can never be disturbed by anything or anyone. That peace then naturally radiates out to everyone else. This alone is true peace, and it cannot be brought about by violent revolutions. As Self-knowledge dawns, even though the personality is retained, the personal identity vanishes into thin air—and with it, the entire story of that person. When the limitations of a person dissolve, limitless peace is all that remains. Life then becomes fulfilled.

॥ इति चतुर्थ खण्डः ॥

iti caturtha khaṇḍaḥ.

Thus ends chapter four.

ॐ सह नाववतु । सह नौ भुनक्तु । सह वीर्यं करवावहै ।
तेजस्विनावधीतमस्तु । मा विद्विषावहै ॥
ॐ शान्तिः शान्तिः शान्तिः

oṁ saha nāvavatu, saha nau bhunaktu, saha vīryaṁ karvāvahai,
tejasvināvadhītamastu, mā vidviṣāvahai.
oṁ śāntiḥ śāntiḥ śāntiḥ

Translation:
Oṁ. May that (divine) protect us both (teacher and student). May that (divine) nourish us both. May we work together with vitality. May our studies be bright. May we never hate each other.
Oṁ, peace, peace, peace.

THE *KENA UPANIṢAD* begins and ends with the same prayer, which perhaps indicates that this study has no end. It is an endless study of that which is limitless…

GLOSSARY

ādhibhautika: physical disturbances in our immediate surroundings

ādhidaivika: natural disturbances

ādhyātmika: inner disturbances from the mind

Ādi Śaṅkarācārya [788-820 CE]: the sage-philosopher who revived the teachings of Advaita Vedānta

advaita: nonduality, non-difference

Advaita Vedānta: the nondual school within the ancient philosophical tradition of Vedānta; its essential teaching is that the world is only an appearance and Consciousness alone is real

Agni: the fire god

ahaṁkāra: ego, the arrogance of individual identity, the feeling "I am this limited person"

amṛta: immortality, deathless; nectar of immortality, a drink that grants immortality to the devas

ānanda: joy, bliss, happiness experienced by abiding in the peace of the Self

anta: end

antaḥstha: a semivowel in Sanskrit

anugraha: grace

anusvāra: a nasal sound in Sanskrit

ardhanārīśvara: an androgynous form of the divine (Śiva and his consort Pārvatī)

asatya: unreal, superficial, false, inauthentic

ashram (āśrama): a spiritual hermitage

asura: a demon, an underground force

ātman: self; one's true nature, the true Self

ātma-vicāra: self-inquiry

avadhūta: an eccentric sage

avagraha: a symbol that is not pronounced but used to indicate prodelision in Sanskrit avatar (avatāra): an embodied form of the divine descended for the upliftment of humanity

avidyā: the ignorance of (or misunderstanding about) one's true nature

Baba (Bābā): father; Swami Muktananda is affectionately known as Baba

Bhagavad Gītā: The Song of God, an ancient sacred text that is in the form of a dialogue between Śrī Kṛṣṇa and Arjuna

Brahman: the divine, supreme principle; pure Consciousness

buddhi: intellect

Chinmayananda, Swami (Cinmayānanda, Svāmī) [1916-1993]: an extraordinary orator and renowned sage who propagated the teachings of Advaita Vedānta; *Chinmayananda* literally means the "joy of Consciousness"

dama: self-control

dantya: a dental consonant in Sanskrit

darśana: vision of the divine

Dattātreya: the first Guru in the lineage of Gurus

deva: a god, a celestial force; divine light

Devanagari (devanāgarī): a script of the Sanskrit language

dhyāna: meditation

dvaita: duality, difference

dveśa: aversion

Guru: a teacher who imparts Self-knowledge

Haimavatī: the daughter of Himavān, one of the names of the goddess Umā who is the consort of Śiva

hatha (haṭha) yoga: the physical postures of yoga

Himavān: the personification of the Himalayas (mountain range); literally, "snowy"

Indra: the king of the gods

japa: mantra repetition

jātaveda: the omniscient one, an epithet of Agni

jñānendriya: the organs of perception (hearing, touching, seeing, tasting, smelling)

kaṇṭhya: a guttural consonant in Sanskrit

karma: the action-reaction principle of nature, action; in this text, selfless action

karmendriya: the organs of action (speech, handling, locomotion, excretion, procreation)

Kashmir Shaivism (Kaśmīra Śaivism): the ancient nondual philosophical tradition that flourished in the region of Kashmir (northern India) and whose essential teaching is that Consciousness alone appears as the world

kathā: a sacred story

kena: by whom?, by what?; the first word of the *Kena Upaniṣad*

kīrtana: group chanting of the name of God

Kṛṣṇa: an avatar, the Guru of Arjuna in the *Bhagavad Gītā*

Lalitā Sahasranāma: The Thousand Names of Lalitā, the goddess

maghavan: the possessor of great wealth, an epithet of Indra

mahābhūta: the great elements (ether, air, fire, water, earth)

mahamandaleshwar (mahāmaṇḍaleśvara): an honorary title bestowed by a group of monks

mahāprāṇa: an aspirated consonant in Sanskrit

mananam: reflection, introspection

mantra: a sacred sound, a sacred syllable, sacred word(s); an *Upaniṣad* verse

mātariśva: the one who treads the skies, an epithet of Vāyu

māyā: the veil that conceals Self-knowledge, the delusion of considering duality as real

mokṣa: freedom from suffering, freedom from the cycle of birth and death

mṛta: death

Muktananda, Baba (Muktānanda, Bābā) [1908-1982]: successor of Bhagavan Nityananda and the world-renowned sage who created a meditation revolution in the 1970s and early 1980s; *Baba* literally means "father," and *Muktananda* literally means the "joy of independence" or the "bliss of freedom"

mūrdhanya: a cerebral consonant in Sanskrit

nāma: a name, a word

Nityananda, Bhagavan (Nityānanda, Bhagavān) [unknown-1961]: the Guru of Baba Muktananda, an eccentric sage (avadhūta) and enlightened being from birth, who settled in the region known as Ganeshpuri (Gaṇeśapurī); *Bhagavan* literally means the "Lord" or the "blessed One," and *Nityananda* literally means "joy of the eternal" or "eternally blissful"

Nityananda, Swami (Nityānanda, Svāmī) [1962-]: successor of Baba Muktananda, and the spiritual head of Shanti Mandir

Oṁ: the divine sound-vibration that permeates every atom of existence

oṣṭhya: a labial consonant in Sanskrit

pāpa: the impressions of past actions and thoughts that keep the individual limited

pluta: an overlong vowel in Sanskrit

pramāṇa: the means of proof

pratibodha: every experience, every thought, every state of consciousness

pratitiṣṭhati: established

Purāṇas: the sacred texts that narrate stories

rāga: attraction

Ramana Maharshi [1879-1950]: the great sage of Arunachala (Aruṇācala) hill who first brought to light in modern times the practice of ātma-vicāra (self-inquiry) by asking the question "Who am I?"; *Maharshi* (maharṣi) literally means a "great sage" ṛṣi: a sage

rūpa: a form, an object

sādhanā: spiritual practice

śakti: the divine, conscious power; inner power, grace, the power of meditation; the divine feminine; the power of Brahman

śaktipāta: the descent (pāta) of grace (śakti), the transmission of grace by a Guru, spiritual awakening

samādhi (shrine): the burial place of a sage

saṁsāra: the cycle of birth and death, rebirth

sanātana: timeless and universal wisdom

śānti: peace

śānti mantra (or śānti pāṭha): a mantra for peace

satya: truth, authenticity; reality

Shanti Mandir (śānti mandira): the spiritual-charitable nonprofit organization founded by Swami Nityananda in 1987; literally, "temple of peace"

Śiva: God, Consciousness, the divine; the god who destroys (individuality); literally, the "auspicious one"

Śiva liṅga: a pillar-like representation of Śiva, usually made of stone

Śiva Sahasranāma: The Thousand Names of Śiva, the god who destroys (individuality)

śraddhā: unquestionable faith

Śrī: an address used to indicate reverence

śruti: that which is heard (*Vedas*)

sūtra: an aphorism

svādhyāya: scriptural study, self-study

svara: a vowel in Sanskrit

svarga: the heaven where devas reside, the land of pleasure

Swami (svāmī): a monk

tadvana: a name for Brahman; literally, the "one who is loved by all"

tālavya: a palatal consonant in Sanskrit

tanmātra: the subtle elements (sound, touch, form or color, taste, smell)

tapa: self-discipline, penance, endurance, tolerance

Umā: a goddess, the consort of Śiva

Upaniṣad: the ultimate knowledge (the knowledge of our true nature); a sacred text (in the *Vedas*) that explores this ultimate knowledge

ūṣma: a sibilant in Sanskrit

Vāyu: the wind god

veda: knowledge

Vedānta: the wisdom found at the end portion (anta) of the *Vedas*; the end (anta) of all knowledge (veda)

*Veda*s: the sacred texts that form the foundation of Vedic or Hindu thought: *Ṛg Veda, Yajur Veda, Sāma Veda,* and *Atharva Veda*

vidyā: knowledge

vīryam: vitality, vigor, inner strength, inner power

visarga: a phone in Sanskrit; literally, "projection"

Viṣṇu Sahasranāma: The Thousand Names of Viṣṇu, the god who preserves (an enlightened engagement with) the world

viveka: the power of discernment

vyañjana: a consonant in Sanskrit

yakśa: a nature-spirit that functions as a guardian of natural wealth; in this text, a mysterious spirit

yoga: union of the individual with the divine

Yoga Sūtras: The Aphorisms on Yoga, an ancient sacred text written by the sage Patañjali that can be considered a textbook of yoga

Recommended Resources

Chinmayananda, Swami. *Kenopanishad.*
Philadelphia: Chinmaya Publications West, 1981.

Six DVDs with talks on the *Kena Upaniṣad* by Swami Chinmayananda in Houston, Texas in 1981. Eloquent and lively lectures on the *Kena Upaniṣad* by an extraordinary orator and renowned sage.

Chinmayananda, Swami. *Kenopaniṣad: Self: Different from Known and Beyond Unknown.*
Mumbai: Central Chinmaya Mission Trust, 2013.

A brilliant translation and commentary.

Gambhirananda, Swami. *Kena Upaniṣad.*
Kolkata: Advaita Ashrama, 1980.

An excellent translation, along with the commentary of Ādi Śaṅkarācārya.

Sharvananda, Swami. *Kena Upanishad.*
Madras: The Ramakrishna Math, 1920.

An excellent translation, with useful comments.

Acknowledgments

I would like to thank Jude Berman for editing the manuscript; Umesh Nagarkatte and Chitra Nagarkatte for checking the Sanskrit, the transliteration, and the translation; and Ron Carter for designing the book.

Foto Corner and Jnaneshwar Gadekar granted permission to use their photographs of Bhagavan Nityananda and Baba Muktananda.

Some material in this book was first printed in *The Speaking Tree* (2016, 2017), a publication of *The Times of India*.

This book would not have been published without the moral support of Devayani, the vice president of Shanti Mandir.

The reflections shared here were fostered in the sacred and powerful environment of Shanti Mandir in upstate New York, one of the ashrams founded by Swami Nityananda, successor of Baba Muktananda.

Mahamandaleshwar Swami Nityananda

Photo: Vasudha Donnelly

About the Author

Vivek grew up in a family of Baba Muktananda's devotees. He holds a BS in biological sciences and a BA in philosophy. After receiving a PhD in molecular biology from Princeton University, he moved into Shanti Mandir's ashram in upstate New York to pursue yoga studies with Sanskrit education full time. He has been teaching yoga philosophy since 2008 and is known for his ability to convey the relevance and practical application of ancient scriptures in our modern lives.

Vivek Desai

Photo: Amita Carpenter

CPSIA information can be obtained
at www.ICGtesting.com
Printed in the USA
FSHW01n1809280918
52401FS

9 781732 142039